Advance Praise for *Sex + Faith*

"Brimming with compassion and  s
Sex + Faith is a love letter to paren el
best to raise kids who love God, th it
down to their X and Y chromos a
teacher shines through on every page, instead of moralizing
she shows *how* parent-child sex conversations, around count-
less topics, might sound at various points in the life cycle—
and how these conversations strengthen the faith of parents
and children alike. *Sex + Faith* doesn't pick ethical fights or
resolve theological disputes (nor does it try to). It's a refresh-
ingly honest, and ultimately hopeful, go-to book that every
parent, children's minister, youth pastor, and educator should
have on their shelves."
—Kenda Creasy Dean, PhD, Professor of Youth, Church
and Culture, Princeton Theological Seminary, and Author
of *Almost Christian: What the Faith of Our Teenagers Is
Telling the American Church* and *The Godbearing Life:
The Art of Soul-Tending for Youth Ministry*

"Good, thoughtful, faithful sex education is probably the best
antidote we have to sexual abuse. Thank God for Kate Ott's
valuable contribution to this effort in our faith communities."
—Rev. Dr. Marie M. Fortune, Founder
and Senior Analyst, FaithTrust Institute

"As a pastor, parent, and person of faith who adamantly
believes the church needs to be more proactive and positive about all matters of sexuality, I applaud and appreciate
everything Kate has presented. From infants to adults, she
has gifted us with a resource that is accessible, engaging, and
sorely needed in our time!"
—Kenji Marui, Coordinating Minister of Worship
and Care, Calvary United Church, Ontario Canada

"Face it, parents need good sexuality education even more
than their kids do, so stand aside Dr. Ruth, Dr. Phil, and Dr.
Spock. Kudos to Kate Ott for writing the book everyone's been
waiting for."
—Rev. Marvin M. Ellison, PhD, Willard Bass Professor
of Christian Ethics, Bangor Theological Seminary

"Intelligent. Faithful. Timely. Every Christian parent and child owes a debt of gratitude to Kate Ott for this grace-filled guide to bringing the good book and the "big talk" into loving and lasting relationship."
—Rev. Dr. Darryl W. Stephens, Clergy,
The United Methodist Church

"Finally, a holistic, 'faith-full' book on sexuality education that isn't only about sex. I wish I had this book when I was raising my two daughters. Explicitly Christian, but values and ethics translate across faiths. A must-read for all parents and grandparents and for anyone working with children and youth."
—Su Yon Pak, EdD, Senior Director & Associate Professor,
Integrative and Field-Based Education, Union Theological
Seminary

"This book is beyond 'user friendly' for parents to teach their children sexuality education. It is a must-read for all who care about bridging the divide between sexuality and faith."
—Evelyn L. Parker, PhD, Associate Professor of Practical
Theology, Perkins School of Theology, Southern Methodist
University

"Kate is faithful, practical, and insightful. She takes the long view that parenting isn't about one-time decisions but about the way parents equip their children to make good choices."
—Dwayne Stinson, Director of Youth Ministries,
Reveille United Methodist Church

"Kate Ott offers an informed, well-written resource that is sensitive to parents' concerns and the complexities of talking with children and teens about sexuality in our time. A terrific resource at any stage of parenting!"
—Joyce Ann Mercer, LCSW, PhD, Professor
of Practical Theology, Virginia Theological Seminary

"Dr. Ott breaks down an important, but sometimes overwhelming, topic into manageable conversations."
—Rev. Micah James, Minister to Families
and Children, Northway Christian Church

Sex + Faith

Talking with Your Child from Birth to Adolescence

KATE OTT

WJK WESTMINSTER
JOHN KNOX PRESS
LOUISVILLE · KENTUCKY

First edition
Published by Westminster John Knox Press
Louisville, Kentucky

13 14 15 16 17 18 19 20 21 22—10 9 8 7 6 5 4 3 2 1

Book design by Erika Lundbom
Cover design by Lisa Buckley

Library of Congress Cataloging-in-Publication Data

Ott, Kate M.
  Sex + faith : talking with your child from birth to adolescence /
Kate Ott. — First edition.
    pages cm
  Includes bibliographical references and index.
  ISBN 978-0-664-23799-8 (alk. paper)
  1. Sex—Religious aspects—Christianity. 2. Sex instruction for children—Religious aspects—Christianity. I. Title. II. Title: Sex and faith.
  BT708.O88 2013
  241'.664--dc23

                                          2013016693

  ♾ The paper used in this publication meets the minimum requirements of the American National Standard for Information Sciences—Permanence of Paper for Printed Library Materials, ANSI Z39.48-1992.

To Brian, for supporting my dreams, keeping me grounded, and always making coffee in the morning . . .

To Eva and Isaac, for asking questions, making me laugh, and helping me pray (correctly) . . .

I am blessed; we are blessed.

Contents

Acknowledgments

B ook writing is a labor of love. For all the critical support and inspiration, I give gratitude to a community of family, friends, colleagues, and youth.

My deepest appreciation goes to my family, who has graciously given me the gift of time when I was away parenting other children in churches across the United States or glued to the chair in front of my computer. To Brian, who brings the potential for co-parenting and healthy relationships to a new standard, not to mention testing out tough sexuality questions with the "Lunch Bunch" at work. Eva and Isaac, you remind me every day that a solid foundation in a faith community, responsibility for others, and love of self can set an example for other children and grown-ups alike.

Many of us benefit from small starts that add up to a larger project and vocation. Over ten years ago, the youth, parents, and wider congregation at Fairfield Grace United Methodist Church inspired me with their confidence, sharing, and determination to create a ministry true to children's and youth's needs. Since then,

I have had the privilege of teaching Sunday school classes and spending time with youth around the country. It is their bravery and honesty in sharing their space and lives with me that undergird this work.

Without wonderful colleagues, the process of writing a book is a lonely prospect. A special thank-you to the Religious Institute, including each of the staff members with whom I have worked, especially Debra Haffner, whose mission and vision allowed me to articulate my own voice. Their work exemplifies how building connections between sexuality, faith, and education is a means to bringing about justice. For the youth ministers who have invited me to their churches, your dedication and foresight in meeting the needs of the youth in your care have compelled me to put the information from the many workshops to (published) paper. I extend special thanks to Molly Kent and Kenji Marui, who read drafts and provided helpful feedback. My appreciation for the tangible and intangible support I have received goes to Shannon Clarkson for reading early drafts and sending me relevant articles and questions; to Melanie Harris, Emilie Townes, Traci West, Angela Sanders, and Jennifer Harvey for supporting my notion of scholarship and activism; and to Kathryn Blanchard, M. T. Davila, Grace Yia-Hei Kao, Rebecca Todd Peters, Elisabeth Vasko, and Aana Marie Vigen for providing scholarly and motherly perspectives throughout the writing process.

Thank you to Westminster John Knox Press for their support in creating a book that brings together Christian theology and sexuality education for the people who need it most—parents and their children. With utter awe and wonder, I thank my editor David Maxwell for believing in the need for this book, the vision for its format, and his close eye in editing. It would only be fitting to also mention the sometimes humorous, always caring challenges of a non-parent editor who asks "why?" just when I thought it was clear. Thank you, David, for the clarity, depth, and brilliance that you have brought to this book.

Introduction

Talking about sex with our children is scary! How do you begin to teach your children about sex when *you* feel so uncomfortable? It is no wonder that so many children get "the talk" from their parents very late in childhood, under awkward circumstances. This plus all the other demands on our time are reasons many parents feel justified in pushing "the talk" down the road.

But it doesn't have to be that way. Our sexuality is a gift from God. It is a natural and amazing part of who we are. Talking about our sexuality and our faith does not need to be tongue twisting or stomach churning for Christian parents. We have good news to share about our faith and our sexuality. This book is a starting point for parents who want to share their faith values as they discuss sexual development, healthy relationships, and sexual decision making with their children.

Here you will find information and new ideas. There are stories in which you might find yourself, your family, or your children's questions reflected. What this book cannot do is take over the job of talking about faith and sexuality with your kids. No book can do that. That is a parent's job as well as the other trusted adults in our children's lives! I know that this is not an easy task. I too stumble through sexuality conversations with my two children. I find it awkward to bring up sexuality issues in my Sunday school classes, and I talk about sexuality for a living! Talking about our faith and beliefs takes practice. Talking about sexuality is no different.

The fact is, as a parent, you are already a sexuality educator, even if you have said nothing about "sex." Your kids are learning by example from how you live in your romantic relationships or lack thereof, how you treat people based on whether they are male or female, how you treat your body and the comments you make about it, and how you show intimacy (or not) through touch such as hugs, kisses, and play with your children.

Each of these lessons also reflects your faith beliefs. Our values are shown by how we treat others and ourselves. Do you express gratitude for the gift of your body? Do you honor others' physical and emotional boundaries? In other words, how we love others and our children teaches them about sexuality and faith without a word being said.

As the first and most important sexuality educator in your child's life, you can talk about the values behind your behaviors and why they are meaningful to you. The examples of behaviors above are left only to the interpretive eyes and ears of our children if adults do not stop and take a moment to reflect on them together. Without stopping to reflect, kids may not always get the most important message or the right one from their observations. Children need and want to hear from their parents.

This book is about taking the next step. As a parent, or one who cares for and guides children in their faith, you can use this book as a map to which you can return throughout your child's life from birth to young adulthood. It has two key sections along with "question boxes" throughout.

Part 1 addresses how Christian faith shapes our understanding of sexuality and parenting. Opportunities abound in daily life to impart information and values to help children become sexually healthy, responsible, and loving adults. It is never too late to teach about sexuality and help them form relationships based on Christian values.

Part 1 also corrects some common myths related to sexuality education and information. In a true-and-false format, these statements are put to the test and often dispelled by current research. Accurate and age-appropriate information will help you feel more confident and ready to answer sexuality-related questions. Yet, no matter how prepared, you will at times be caught off guard by a question from a child. A process is suggested for answering these sorts of questions in chapter 6, "Steps for Answering Children's Questions."

Part 2 is organized according to age ranges. Each chapter begins with a short parenting quiz to test your sexuality IQ related to major developmental milestones for that age group. As with any categorization, these age groupings are not perfect, and each merits an entire book. Indeed, there are other resources that are age-specific and where possible, additional ones will be mentioned. Each chapter briefly describes the stages of physical, faith, and relationship development, including typical issues experienced. Each chapter also has a "Connecting Faith and Sexuality Education" section with suggested Bible stories or church practices for the age. The chapters end with a quick replay of the top educational moments and messages for parents' quick reference.

A number of question boxes are interspersed throughout the book as sidebars or shaded pages. They lead with a question that parents might ask or something a child might say or ask. The answers are brief and to the point, and some offer reference to an organization or Web site for more information.

My hope is that you enjoy reading this book and use it as a reference throughout your child's growth and development. All parents need companions in raising children. That does not necessarily mean being married or partnered. Companions include good resources and a host of other adults to help! This book focuses on how sexuality education, parenting, and faith intersect.

Consider sharing this book with grandparents, teachers, and trusted adults in your child's life so that they can also share sexuality-related messages, values, and faith beliefs. I recommend that you also get a separate series of age-related books on sexual health for you and your children. There are many good resources, and some are listed in the "Additional Resources" section at the end of the book.

Finally, a note about the author: me. I worked for five years as the Children and Youth Minister in a large parish prior to becoming a professor of Christian Ethics at a small seminary in the Northeast, Drew Theological School. I continue to serve as a middle school Sunday school teacher. In addition to training clergy and youth ministers, I travel the country leading youth and parenting workshops on faith values and sexuality education. I began working in churches over fifteen years ago, and I continue to learn new things each year about sexuality, faith, and parenting. This book is based on my experience and research. It is regularly tested and tweaked by the children, teens, and parents I have met when speaking at churches, not to mention in my own home where my husband and I parent our elementary- and middle school-aged children.

PART 1

The Big Picture

Chapter 1

Five Common Myths

When it comes to talking about sexuality, we all have different experiences. Yet many parents share some common assumptions, such as:

+ My child is too young to understand.
+ Once I explain how babies are made, my job is done.
+ Talking about sexuality leads to experimentation.
+ I must have all the answers.
+ I can do this in one talk.

Each of these is based in a genuine concern for doing a good job as a parent and for protecting the well-being of our children. We have a desire to protect them, to give them accurate information, and to let them live a carefree life away from the "big problems" of adults for as long as possible. Unfortunately, that parental instinct is counter to what our children need. Kids need accurate, age-appropriate information so that they can know and honor their bodies, create healthy relationships with friends and romantic partners, and confidently say no now, and yes later to sexual behaviors.

Myth #1: My Child Is Too Young to Understand

When adults talk about sexuality, we do so with our adult glasses on. It is only natural. All our past experiences and knowledge inform what we know about sexuality. These can mislead us when talking with our children. For example, a two-year-old girl walks in on her naked father and asks, pointing to his penis, "Daddy, what's that?" Looking through his adult glasses, the father's reaction includes concerns of overexposure ("Did I freak my girl out?"), breach of privacy ("Got to get a lock on that door!"), having to talk about what a penis is used for ("Oh God, help me!"), why boys have them and girls do not ("Ah, this is only for boys."), concern that the child might tell a teacher today in preschool what she saw ("Yes, Ms. X that did happen, but it's not what it sounds like."), and on and on. In fact, in the child's mind, "What's that?" is really all she wants to know because she doesn't have one.

We need to take our adult glasses off and answer her question. "Are you talking about my penis? That is a part of the body that boys have. As a girl, you have a vulva." At this point, if you do have a closed-door privacy policy in your house, you might add: "Remember, we knock at the door before coming in because grown-ups get privacy when they are getting dressed." In that simple exchange, you have acknowledged that you are comfortable with your body and she should be with hers, privacy is important at different times for different people, and you will answer questions that she has; also, these were accomplished in an age-appropriate and accurate manner.

More so than with any other subject about life, parents often provide too little, too late when it comes to talking about sexuality with their children. Study after study shows that when teens are asked what they learned as children and what they would have liked to have learned about sexuality, they complain about knowing too little. Part 2 of this book will help you with information for your child's age and development.

When we take off our adult glasses and recognize our children's questions for what they are, we do no harm by sharing information. We may actually do the exact opposite. We are keeping them safe. For example, the correct names for body parts may keep a child safe by being able to report and identify sexual abuse. Knowing how pregnancy occurs and how sexually transmitted infections (STIs) are transmitted may persuade a teenager to choose not to engage in such behaviors and know how to protect themselves if they do. Knowledge does not cause harm; it is the touchstone to empowering our children to lead healthy, faithful, and safe lives. In fact, kids often understand much more than we give them credit, and if parents are not sharing information then kids could be learning it from less-reliable sources.

Myth #2: Once I Explain How Babies Are Made, My Job Is Done

Sexuality includes much more than sexual intercourse and reproduction. Many adults reduce all of what sexuality encompasses into just one behavior. Certainly the media, Christianity's fixation on the act of sex, and the wonderful pleasure and fruitfulness that can come from it, have all built the pedestal on which sexual intercourse sits in our minds. This again is an *adult glasses* view. Children do not know what sexual intercourse is until either we or some kid on the playground informs them.

Sexuality encompasses relationships, our bodies, what it means for us to be a boy or a girl (gender identity and roles), and, yes, occasionally sexual intercourse. Chances are you are already having a lot of conversations related to sexuality without calling it that.

Myth #3: Talking about Sexuality Leads to Experimentation

The opposite is true. Research has found that providing information is actually empowering for decision making and may help kids delay sexual behaviors.[1] Information is not permission giving. With the Internet and the amount of time kids spend in afterschool programs, they already know a lot about sexuality. In order for your kids to connect their faith values with sexuality information, parents and religious education programs need to talk about sexuality.

If we withhold or delay sexuality information, sexuality education becomes a "history lesson" for kids. Consider the fact that close to half of teens who are engaging in sexual intercourse report that they did not have information about contraception prior to their first time. They were unprepared. You wouldn't let your child drive your car without taking driver's education class and building up their comfort level. Sharing sexuality information is about providing comfort and increasing safety and prevention.

Myth #4: I Must Have All the Answers

Nine out of ten parents suffer from "performance anxiety." As adults and as parents, we often believe that we should have all the right answers before attempting to talk about sex with our kids. There is nothing wrong with not knowing the answer to one of their questions. In fact, it is a great lesson for children when a parent says, "I don't know the answer to that. Let's go look it up." Or "Can I get back to you?" Then make sure to get back to your child with the information. If you don't, it sends a signal that this is not a topic to be shared. We are all lifelong learners, even about sexuality. That is a positive message.

There is no magic pill for performance anxiety. Reading this book and browsing suggested Web sites will help. But the best medicine is to practice with your child starting right now. Ideally you can begin when your child is young with easier topics. They are a less critical audience and more likely to listen than your teenager. Naming body parts correctly or talking about different types of kisses and hugs can build up parental confidence and ease. If a child is older and you are just beginning, practice responding to questions with a partner or a family friend to gain comfort. Think of those difficult questions your child may ask, including personal questions about drug or alcohol use. Practice what you will say if your child asks, "When is the first time you had sex?" (see page 111 for ways to answer this). Being good at anything takes practice. Parenting is no exception!

Myth #5: I Can Do This in One Talk

You may remember "the talk" or getting a book from your parents. When my mother decided to tell me about sexual intercourse and pregnancy, I was relieved because a girlfriend had recently made a comment about my classmate's pregnant mother unzipping her stomach to have her baby. I knew that was wrong, but honestly did not know why. I remember two things about my unforgettable mother-daughter talk:

+ *The context:* We were in a dimly lit room with the door closed.
+ *The fact:* Babies come out between a woman's legs, not from a zipper on her stomach.

I do not remember 90 percent of the other facts my mother told me that evening. Yet I remember the context in ways I imagine she did not intend. My dimly lit birds-and-bees discussion reinforced for me that sexuality was a secret, private matter to be talked about behind closed doors, with my mother (not my father), and was only going to happen once. I had to wait until a fifth grade school assembly to watch the "girls only" video and hear the visiting nurse tell me what I had missed.

What I did learn from my mother's well-meaning "talk" is an important reminder for me as a parent:

+ It isn't just what we say that makes a difference. The context speaks volumes.
+ The facts are fleeting. Kids need more than one talk. They

need many little talks that sexuality educators call "teach-able moments."

+ Just because kids don't ask questions, doesn't mean they don't have them.
+ If you do not provide the information, most kids will find it elsewhere. It may be incorrect, and it definitely won't be set in the context of your family values.

On a more positive note, my parents were providing me with many other lessons related to sexuality whether they knew it or not. They taught me and my siblings about how to be in loving, long-term relationships and work through times of joy and conflict. They were affectionate to each other and to us. They were always present for us and loved us by supporting our schooling, work, and friends—even if we did not always appreciate it. Our church community and faith were an integral part of our family life and often informed the rules by which our family lived. In other words, there was consistency between faith teachings and practices related to my parents' understanding of marriage, dating, and sexual behaviors. They might have been uncomfortable talking about sexual behaviors and sexuality in general, but they lived their beliefs in a way that taught us about qualities of a healthy relationship like mutuality, trust, and love.

Our children and teenagers need sexuality education that is honest and age-appropriate and is set in the context of Christian values of respect, responsible caring, and love for self, others, and God. They deserve sexuality education that addresses all aspects of sexuality.

Chapter 2

The Parent's Role

A parent includes any and all those amazing individuals who take on the challenge and gift of raising children. Parents come in a variety of shapes and sizes, including adoptive, single, heterosexual and gay/lesbian couples, grandparents, extended family, legal guardians, and so on. Ministers, teachers, coaches, and Christian educators also share responsibility for parenting children. No matter the composition of our families, most parents want to help their children grow in positive self-esteem, learn limit-setting, and make choices based on faith values. Each of these is an important part of developing a healthy sexuality and forming healthy relationships.

Parenting that promotes healthy development is more about finesse and balance than rules or step-by-step plans. Raising kids is not like assembling furniture or hooking up a new computer with one-size-fits-all directions that, when followed correctly, result in a working product. There is no magical word or set of information to be said at one perfect moment. Instead, parents can begin by giving kids tools to use throughout life to meet the various challenges that they will face. Those tools include faith practices and values as well as interpersonal skills and information (mentioned in the next chapters). The combination equips children to work through problems, form meaningful relationships, and know that they are supported and loved as they do so.

Q&A

I'm divorced and my "ex" holds the exact opposite position on everything. What should I do?

Consistent positive messages about sexuality contribute to children becoming sexually healthy adults. But kids are inundated with a variety of sexuality messages every day that come from grown-ups and friends. Helping your children to be good decision makers means helping them take different opinions and discern which fits their values best. Being clear about differences is honest, not contradictory.

The Christian concept of stewardship helps describe the role of parents. We are stewards of our children. The most popular model of parenting seems to change every week, from helicopter parent to the tiger moms. The Christian stewardship model is constant and time tested. Below are three statements that explain what parenting as a practice of stewardship means.

#1: Parents Raise Children; They Do Not Own Children

Parents are given children to raise and nurture as important members of God's creation. The basic concept of stewardship is taking care of or managing someone else's things. In the Christian tradition, stewardship means something more than just meeting basic needs of food, shelter, reading, and writing. Because we are created in the image of God, all human beings—regardless of their race, gender, orientation, family origin, education, and so on—have God-given dignity and worth that are to be nurtured.

God entrusts us to be stewards of our children. Thus, parenting requires us to take care of our children not for personal benefit, but so they realize their worth and dignity and responsibilities as members of God's creation.

#2: Parents Share Their Responsibility; They Are Not the Only Stewards of Their Children

Parents are the first educators and primary stewards, but stewardship as parenting means kids are not only *not* ours but also need *other* parents as well. One or two grown-ups cannot provide all the stewardship a child needs to become a faithful adult who contributes to a greater good. We need God and others to help. Similar to any parenting issue, sexuality education is not something that parents can, nor must, do on their own. Children and youth need other "ask-able adults" as well as consistent messages about sexuality and faith values from those they trust, such as grandparents, clergy, teachers, and so on. Intergenerational examples of healthy and loving relationships in the context of a faith community offer kids lessons about sexuality that parents and one family structure cannot provide. They may also be people your child turns to with questions about sexuality when they are not comfortable asking you.

Q&A

I've been the worst example for my child. Who am I to teach him/her anything?

One of the best ways to teach children is by example. That example doesn't need to be perfect. In fact, explaining your past mistakes or why you think you made bad choices may help kids understand the consequences of their actions.

#3: Parents Model Values with Their Behavior; They Do Not Only Teach with Words

"Practice what you preach" is not just an adage. Moral development literature tells us that primarily it is what you do, not what you say, that contributes to how our kids learn to make choices based on their faith values. Stewardship is about mentoring and role modeling through our own practices. It is a process, not an end goal. The Christian stewardship model of parenting starts kids on the path to becoming faithful adults. For kids to truly accept faith values as their own, they need to engage in a process of challenging values, sifting through ideas, and finding their place in the world. This process is called moral discernment or development (the second part will deal with specific changes for each age group). Our support encourages formation of their values, not as rules given to them, but as values discovered and lived out by them. It is what faith communities and individuals have been doing throughout history. As Christian stewards, we are entrusted to manage God's gifts in this world. What an awesome responsibility! What a challenging opportunity!

Chapter 3

The Faith Connection

Faith helps kids understand and deal with developmental changes in their bodies and their relationships. Our faith is made up of particular beliefs, formed in a community and supported by specific practices. For Christians, faith includes believing that we are loved by God and trusting in God's will. We believe this to be true regardless of logical or material proof. As one of my friends is fond of saying, "God's love claims me, and I could not imagine it any other way." Out of this belief we develop ways of explaining how we know God loves us and what God's plan is in the world. We do this when we point to the Bible as our faith story, when we form faith communities with specific doctrines, and when we engage in specific practices like prayer, sacraments, and rites of passage.

Our faith influences our parenting, friendships, and romantic relationships. As parents, we hope that faith values will be a source of strength, direction, and comfort to our children as they navigate the generally wavy, sometimes treacherous, and occasionally calm waters of puberty.

Faith is a type of compass that provides direction, but not specific answers. There are a number of ways that we become more specific about our faith: by adopting specific beliefs (theologies), joining a particular community (denominations); and relying on similar practices (congregational life).

Christians hold many of these beliefs, community structures, and practices in common. They help inform not only how parents think about sexuality and relationships, but what children learn through specific teachings and also through observing and participating in a faith community. Obviously, there are too many ways to name here, but other ideas are shared throughout the age-related chapters in the sections titled "Faith Development" and "Connecting Faith and Sexuality Education." In addition, there are recommended readings on faith and sexuality in the resource list at the end of this book.

Core Christian Beliefs

God Is Love

God values us for who we are. When the world seems always to want something different or more from us, we can turn to God and know that we are enough. A caring, devoted child-parent relationship helps to model unconditional love, but we are human and have our moments. Kids need to know that God's abiding and affirming love is always there for them. God also forgives and is a God of second chances. This can be sustaining for children and parents when other relationships are confusing or broken.

God's relationship with us allows for freedom of choice, but also requires a certain level of responsibility. It isn't controlling or "anything goes." We strive for healthy balance in our relationship with God, something that carries through to our other relationships. Also, God loves us for who we are, not what we look like or how many awards we win and good grades we get. This can be a needed boost for self-esteem when we feel unloved by the world's (our parent's or peer's) standards.

Jesus Was Human and Divine

The Christian tradition believes that Jesus was fully human and fully divine. That means our God understands what it means to live in a body with all its limitations as well as its beauty. Jesus ate with his followers, washed with them, woke up with sleep in his eyes, and was dunked under water for his baptism. These are all things that require a body to be enjoyed.

Jesus—our God—experienced the pleasure of touch when his mother held him, when his friends greeted him, when Mary anointed him. He also experienced violence to his body when he was beaten and crucified. The incarnation (Jesus' becoming fully human) shows us that our bodies are wonderful and integral to how we experience and know the world and live in relationships. Our sexuality is part of who we are as human bodies. It was the same for Jesus.

Scripture Teaches about God and How to Live

Scripture can provide children with a map or guide that we use to discern what God asks of us. When I say it is a map or guide, I mean Scripture grounds us in a historical family that's trying to figure out the perennial faith question: what does God ask of me? Scripture is about people who lived long ago in a different cultural time. There may be specific things that we learn about in Scripture that we should not repeat, including some horrible sexuality-related stories like rape, women being silent, and discussion about equality in marriage and specific sexual behaviors. Scripture gives us the big picture of God's relationship with a holy people and Jesus' ministry as an example for Christian practice.

The biblical story teaches us at least two fundamental lessons about sexuality and relationships. First, God created us and that includes our sexuality. Second, the greatest commandment includes caring for others, which means caring for them sexually as well.

> Then God said, "Let us make humankind in our image, according to our likeness." (Gen. 1:26)

> God saw everything that [God] had made, and indeed, it was very good. (Gen. 1:31)

Christians believe that our bodies are part of God's beautiful creation. Sexuality is part of who we are and, just like the rest of what God created, it is good. Because it is good we need to understand it and treat it with care. Ways we care for our bodies include: learning about and preparing for bodily changes; using protection to prevent sexually transmitted infections (STIs) or unintended pregnancy; embracing differences (including physical and mental disabilities) as signs of God's diverse creation; and not objectifying or using our (or others') bodies in disrespectful and demeaning ways.

> He Answered: "You shall love the Lord your God with all your heart, and with all your soul, and with all your strength, and with all your mind; and your neighbor as yourself." (Luke 10:27)

The greatest commandment instructs us to love and treat each other as we would like to be treated. If parents can instill this sense of respect for others in their children, the child will make the connections in their sexual relationships as they develop.

Faith Community

Faith communities provide one of the only intergenerational learning places for our children. Today it is difficult to learn from each other across the generations as extended families are spread around the country and activities are limited to age groups, such as kid events, parents' night out, singles' ministries, and older adult care and missions. We know kids learn through example. Kids need to see multiple examples of how people of all ages model healthy and loving relationships within their faith values.

At times faith communities might expect a little too much of kids, but that future expectation and clear message about God's purpose for them contributes significantly to their decision making. Kids are less likely to engage in risk-taking behavior if they understand that their lives have a greater purpose and if they know a community supports their future success.

A final word of caution. Intergenerational and diverse faith communities can be invaluable experiences for all. Unfortunately, Christians are not perfect, and we have a special obligation to keep children safe from abuse, violence, and harm as they develop life-giving and life-enhancing relationships with God, themselves, and each other. Most churches have realized this, given some high-profile clergy abuse scandals, and put safeguards into place to protect children from potential sexual predators. Ask leaders in your faith community what sexual abuse prevention policies and education are part of the children's and family ministries.

Faith Practices

Prayer

Prayer is talking to God one-on-one or in community. Prayers might be a set of words that we say the same every time (like the Lord's Prayer, Hail Mary, or a meal prayer); an open conversation; body movement (like meditation or liturgical dance); or intentional listening. No matter the format a prayer takes, it is intended to foster communication between God and us. Prayer allows us to tell God what's going on, to practice reflecting on our lives, and to build the most important relationship in our lives—all things that will help us build healthy relationships with others. Additionally, as a child and especially a teenager, having another place to turn with one's problems and joys, no matter how small, is significant.

Rites of Passage

All faith communities celebrate rites of passage. Some may be associated with sacraments and ceremonies like baptism, Communion, confirmation, or marriage. Others mark a transition in age and ability, like receiving a children's Bible in third grade or a study Bible in seventh grade. These rites of passage often take place around key transitions in one's sexual and relational development. They communicate to a child or youth that they have reached a different stage in their relationship with God and others, and we prayerfully trust that they are ready for new experiences. Because we are sexual beings from birth to death and in relationships our whole lives, rites of passage help us honor how our sexuality and relationships change over time. This is an extremely important lesson to learn when it comes to long-term relationships. We will not be the same person or have the same sexual experiences when we are twenty as when we are forty or sixty or eighty. But, difference and change do not need to be seen as problems; rather we can celebrate them.

Of course, like many parents, I want my children to share my faith beliefs, community, and practices. Up to a certain age, I can probably enforce that. However, teaching kids to be good decision makers and faithful people means letting them question their parents' faith beliefs and practices. Faith that is forced is not really faith. We can take time to explain to our children what *our* faith has to do with *our* ideas about sexuality and relationships. We also lead best by example.

Chapter 4

What Exactly Is *Sexuality* Education?

Sexuality education means learning about all aspects of sexuality and how it changes throughout our lifetime. It is a lifelong process of learning. Like other forms of education, we learn by example, through experience, and from direct information in the form of books, Web sites, and conversations. Sexuality is a very complex part of who we are. Faith beliefs and teachings shape and guide what we think about our bodies and how we act in relationships. This learning process begins early between parents and children, siblings, and friends. It is a developmental process toward self-understanding, but also toward sexual health and wholeness.

At all ages and developmental stages, we need to care for and respect our bodies and practice building and maintaining relationships. For example, at age two we learn to wash hands, hug gently, or ask before touching someone else's body. At age eleven, we start to use deodorant, take more frequent showers, sustain multiple friendships even when these friends are not friends with each other, and respond to parents in respectful and reciprocal ways. At age twenty, sexual health and wholeness might include using contraception and STI protection, communicating openly with a partner about sexual pleasure, maintaining enduring friendships while exploring romantic relationships, and establishing mutual communication channels with parents.

Many sexuality educators define holistic sexuality using five broad categories:

1. *Sexual health and reproduction* is the biology and physiology of our bodies and the sexual and reproductive systems, including how we care for our bodies, health consequences of sexual behavior, and the biology of reproducing. This includes sexual behaviors, physical changes in puberty or menopause, infertility, sexual dysfunction, contraception, HIV/AIDS, sexually transmitted infections (STIs), and more.

2. *Sensuality* is how our bodies respond to pleasure, primarily through our senses. This includes our body image and perceptions of our body. It is not only how our bodies experience pleasure but also how we understand and respond to those experiences.

3. *Intimacy* is emotional closeness to another person or God and having that closeness reciprocated. Intimacy includes emotions like trust, vulnerability, and love as they are lived out in relationships to our family, friends, romantic partners, and God.

4. *Sexual identity* is often understood on continuums including who we are as male or female (sex), what masculine or feminine qualities we have (gender identity), how we fit into what society says a boy or girl should be (gender role), and to whom we are attracted (sexual orientation). See "Some Helpful Definitions" on page 22 for a more in-depth discussion of sexual and gender identity.

5. *Sexualization* is the use of sexual behaviors or sexuality to influence or control. Sexualization is not necessarily

negative. Think about flirting as a use of sexuality. Yet, the negative aspects of sexualization do seem pervasive in our culture. Sexualization can happen on an individual level in the case of bullying based on gender or orientation and by withholding sex to punish or to get something in return. On a societal level, we see sexualization at work in advertising, movies, and television.

Sexuality education addresses information, experiences, and changes that relate to all five areas. Since our understanding of sexuality is shaped by the time and space in which we live, it is constantly unfolding and changing as we develop physically, emotionally, and spiritually. Messages in our culture and history can tell us many different, conflicting, and at times unhealthy ways to understand sexuality. Those messages change with age. They may also be different based on our racial/ethnic background, gender identity, geographic location, or cultural and religious surroundings to name a few influences.

Q&A

I'm uncomfortable discussing sexuality with my child. What can I do to get over that?

Practice, practice, practice. Call on a friend or your partner to ask you sexuality-related questions and practice your responses. Start out with small steps like getting a book to share with your child or talking about a sexuality event on TV like a character kissing another person.

Our sexuality develops in and through relationships with self, God, others, and even creation—in moments like a hug from our parent after we fall off a bike, enjoyment of the warm sun on our face, the joy of seeing a familiar friend, talking about our feelings to a friend or partner. Our sexuality is silenced and we feel shame in moments when a parent dismisses our question about where babies come from, an adult tells us not to touch "down there," we are not prepared for menstruation or nocturnal emission, a friend or lover betrays us by lying, or we are forced or coerced to engage in sexual behaviors. Part of sexuality education is helping children develop relationships skills. Here are five developmental skills that can promote loving, healthy relationships:

#1: Self-Confidence

Nurturing children's self-confidence enables them to make decisions based on their own beliefs and values, meaning they are less likely to be swayed by peer pressure. This backfires a bit in toddlerhood and the teenage years. However, self-confidence is well worth the strong-headedness that might come as a byproduct.

#2: Communication Skills

The ability to articulate feelings and decisions helps any relationship to function more smoothly, whether it is with peers, teachers, parents, or a new acquaintance. Communication involves being able to talk with others, listen, and respond as well as understand how our body language sends messages.

#3: Decision-Making Skills

We often raise children with too many choices or too few choices. Kids need to practice decision making with limited choices that give them the opportunity to explore possibilities and weigh consequences. Parents can also model decision making by sharing why and how they make decisions.

#4: Knowledge and Facts (Safety and Prevention)

Information is power. For example, knowing what to expect the first day of school helps a child relax, gain confidence, and be prepared. This is especially true about sexual development and behaviors. Yet, things do not always go as expected. In that case, information related to who to call or how to find help prevents further problems and could keep us safe.

#5: Patience

Patience is an important ingredient to all healthy relationships. Imagine parenting or loving without patience. Impossible! Some of us have more patient personalities; some of us need to learn patience. In a world where we can usually get what we want when we want it, the practice of patience is essential. It balances stubbornness, enables communication, and helps kids learn that sometimes waiting is the best option.

+   +   +

Some Helpful Definitions

Sexuality is a unique and special part of who God created us to be; we should communicate about it in positive and affirming ways whenever we talk with our kids. We can do this by being prepared. That means we have to be clear about what we mean by different sexuality-related terms. In addition to the definition of sexuality provided earlier in this chapter, here are a few terms about our sexual and gender identity that you might find helpful.

Sex: This term describes whether someone is male, female, or intersex. Sex is determined by biological factors such as hormones, chromosomes, internal sex organs, and external genitalia.

Sexual Orientation: By this term we mean our attraction or desires toward others; it is often identified as homosexual, heterosexual, or bisexual. Men who are attracted to men often use the term *gay* and women who are attracted to women may use the term *lesbian.* What shapes our attraction and desire is heavily researched and without conclusive findings. We do know that people may experience sexual desire, romantic love, and build friendships across a spectrum of male and female relationships.

Queer: This can be a derogatory term that has historically been used to refer to gay men and lesbians. Many people have sought to reclaim the term as a way to describe sexual orientation (attractions and desires) that do not fit neatly into heterosexual, homosexual, or bisexual categories. In some cases, queer is used to describe any identity, thinking, or behavior that does not fit within a binary system (meaning only two options) regarding gender (masculine/feminine), sex (male/female), or orientation (heterosexual/homosexual). See below for the term *genderqueer.*

Gender: How one understands and expresses their masculine and feminine feelings, behaviors, and appearance forms their gender identity.

Gender Roles: This refers to the socially defined (and expected) feminine and masculine characteristics and behaviors that one ought to feel and express based on their sex (e.g., males should not cry, females should take care of children).

Transgender: Someone whose sex does not match the corresponding socially expected gender roles or someone whose sex does not match their gender identity is transgender. For example, females who wear men's clothes, act in masculine stereotypical roles, or use masculine pronouns such as *he* to refer to themselves. Others might not present or identify with either or any gender. There are many different variations on the definition of transgender. Some people refer to it as an umbrella term that includes people who cross-dress and transsexual adults who have had surgery to change their genitals and/or hormones to alter their secondary sex characteristics, such as facial hair and breast tissue. The use of *trans* as a prefix suggests moving between (or even beyond) the two poles of gender identity.

Gender Variant: This is a clinical term used to describe children who behave like and report feeling that their sex does not match their gender identity. This is not a tomboy or tomgirl in the sense that a child plays or acts in ways that do not consistently match expected gender roles for their sex. Gender-variant children fit within the transgender umbrella and may elect for hormone suppression as they move through puberty.

Genderqueer: This identification moves beyond masculine and feminine descriptions of gender and plays with gender-role expectations. Individuals who identify as genderqueer do not feel that the categories of man, woman, or transgender fit their self-understanding.

For more terms and their ever-changing definitions, visit the terms section of the Sex, etc. Answers program Web site at Rutgers University, accessed at http://www.sexetc.org.

Chapter 5

What's Changed Since I Was a Kid?

The answer is some things, but not all. Even though you had to walk ten miles to school uphill both ways and kids now get picked up at their front door by the bus, many things have remained the same about childhood and teenage years. Sexual developmental (how our bodies change) has remained mostly the same since the 1900s. Sexual orientation (who we are attracted to) has remained relatively consistent in adult self-reported studies, we are just more open to allowing people to live in relationships that affirm their orientation and may notice it more. The age at which people first engage in sexual intercourse has remained fairly consistent over the past fifty years with little dips or peaks, but no radical changes. Each of these suspected changes will be dealt with in turn below.

What has changed is how much independence our children have. Even a generation or two ago, children had more freedom to move about their neighborhoods, take responsibility for chores, and gain employment. There are also parenting trends that limit how often children are able to control their decisions, friendships, and responsibilities. Many parents choose to or have to work longer hours, meaning that kids are often in day-care or afterschool programs and are therefore under adult supervision most if not all of their day. When we are home, we keep kids in our sights at all times: they sit inside and watch more television and they have playdates instead of roaming the neighborhood with friends. Because of these changes, parents need consciously to create opportunities for children to practice independence.

Yes, things have changed, but not as much as we think! Let's take on some of the myths of child development as they relate to sexuality.

True or False? Kids go through puberty sooner than their parents' generation.

False and true. Menarche (beginning of menstruation), sper-marche (development of sperm in testicles), and semenarche (first ejaculation) have not changed much for the past 50 years. However, secondary sex characteristic development (breasts, hair, lowering of voice, and so forth) is beginning earlier in the United States. Studies suggest that a higher fat diet contributes to earlier onset of secondary sex characteristics. There are also differences in development across racial/ethnic groups. Early secondary sex characteristic development is not a medical health issue (however, causal factors such as childhood obesity should be taken seriously). Yet the social response of adults and older children to a fully developed nine-year-old girl or boy has been proven to have psychological effects on children. Imagine being a ten-year-old girl in fourth grade, looking like a sixteen-year-old and being treated like one at the mall, from the clothes available to the response of young male passersby. These are subtle and not so subtle forms of sexualization that can impact the develop-ing body image and other aspects of sexuality if this is not openly discussed.

True or False? Sexualized music and media are corrupting children's innocence.

False. The answer is false, but with a caveat. Since the radio waves in the 1950s played rock 'n' roll (and probably before that even), parents have thought media was corrupting their children. Every day it seems the news boasts of a new study that suggests kids watch too much TV, play too many video games, and have hearing loss from loud music and headphone use. Kids (and adults) use more technology than ever before. Technology itself is not bad. Related to sexuality, the real question is what is the quality of the media and the parental involvement in consuming that media?

It is *true* that media and music are more sexualized than they have been in the past, meaning there are more sexual images and behaviors.[1] Research does show that sexualized images, specifically of girls, are viewed by children of a younger age and may have a negative effect on young girls' self-esteem, desire to receive elective cosmetic surgery, and early sexual behaviors. Given that about three-fourths of all television shows that youth are viewing contain sexual content and only one-third of the time they reference the risk or responsibility of sexual activity, parents need to understand which TV shows their children are watching and engage in conversation with their children about these shows.[2] Teaching children the skills to be tech savvy and discerning consumers will help them throughout their lives.

Common Sense media is a great parent resource to review the latest movie, TV show, or music video. Their writers raise issues parents could discuss with kids prior to or while watching certain shows. See http://www.commonsensemedia.org/.

True or False? Kids get all their sexuality information from the Internet.

False. Most surveys report that teens get their information from their parents, usually mothers.[3] Doctors, teachers, and friends are a close second. However, the Internet can be a good place to go for sexual health information. It can also be a parent's worst nightmare. Knowing what sites your child visits and having the computer in a central area when kids are young is an important part of teaching Web-based skills and safety practices. As kids get older, they are on the computer at school, on their phones, and at friends' houses. Rather than have them surf the Internet and fear what might pop up, we can provide our tweens and teens with informative, accurate, and age-appropriate sites. A good site for kids is the Answers program at Rutgers University (http://answer.rutgers.edu/) and their peer education site (http://www.sexetc.org).

True or False? All teenagers are having sex, except mine.

False, and maybe true. Very few young teens engage in sexual intercourse.[4] By the time they are seniors in high school, over half of teens have engaged in sexual intercourse.[5] These numbers change only slightly based on geographic region and racial/ethnic identity. Since the 1950s, 90 percent of married people have reported that they engaged in sexual intercourse prior to marriage.[6] When it comes to sexual behaviors and relationships, teens aren't engaging in sexual behaviors that much earlier or often than their parents' generation. The difference is that in the past people usually had sexual intercourse with the person they were going to marry, and that marriage took place only a year or two after high school. Now, most people do not form long-term or life commitments until they are in their late twenties. This means that there is a longer period of time between first intercourse and finding a long-term partner. In the United States today, young adults (under age twenty-four) on average have two to three partners with whom they have had sexual intercourse.[7]

True or False? There are more gay and lesbian teens than when I was in high school.

False (probably). Few longitudinal studies exist on gay and lesbian identification among teens. Other studies do not provide helpful comparisons as some ask about sexual behaviors, sexual desires, or self-identification. For example, if a teenage girl kisses another girl at a party, she would report that she engaged in a sexual behavior with a person of the same sex, but this is not self-identification as lesbian and may not relate to her sexual orientation at all. What is true is that more teens are self-identifying and "coming out" earlier.[8] Attitudes in the United States are changing with regard to acceptance of gay, lesbian, bisexual, and even transgender teens and adults. Thus, we see and know more kids and adults who are openly gay and lesbian. In many schools, this has been supported by student-led gay-straight alliances that promote education and acceptance of lesbian, gay, bisexual, transgender, and queer (LGBTQ) teens. However, bullying related to sexual orientation and gender identity is a major issue for many kids.[9] The resource section at the end of this book contains Web sites and organizations for LGBTQ teens and their parents.

True or False? Kids don't date anymore.

False . . . and true. The answer depends on the definition of dating. While dating practices like going to dinner and a movie or securing a prom date months in advance are no longer the norm, teens and young adults still "date." That is, they have a significant other with whom friends and acquaintances know they are paired. Sometimes they do things alone, but for the most part they travel in groups of friends or meet up somewhere. For some past generations, dating in high school was a mating ritual leading up to a marriage proposal. The timing, purpose, and necessity for marriage have changed due to economic and cultural shifts. In a domino effect, the purpose of dating has changed as well. Dating is for companionship, expressing and fulfilling sexual desires, learning to build relationships, and falling in love—the end goal doesn't always have to be marriage.

For young adults, the phenomenon of "hooking up" can also dramatically shift dating rituals. Hooking up is characterized by meeting people in group situations and pairing off to engage in various levels of sexual behaviors. Generally, there are no strings attached—meaning neither person intends a romantic relationship to develop.

One may hook up with lots of different people or the same person a few times. The key to hooking-up is that there are no expectations of caring for the other person; wanting a relationship with them; or more precisely, wanting the hard work of developing a relationship. Of course, this often appears to participants to be a good idea in theory, but in practice it is often very emotionally messy. Many teens and current young adults express a desire to bring back "the good" parts of dating culture like structured time to get to know each other, adding different types of sexual behaviors over time, and exclusivity from the start. Still, they would like to leave behind "outdated" practices that promote gender inequality, waiting for sexual intercourse until marriage, and the notion that everyone you date is someone you will potentially marry.[10]

Chapter 6

Steps for Answering Children's Questions

K ids say the darndest things! They also ask really great questions. Answering their questions in a concise, informative, and supportive manner invites them to keep asking questions from the time they are toddlers until they are teenagers (maybe even longer). Sexuality education is a two-way street. Parents can use "teachable moments" to discuss sexuality issues; they don't need to wait around for questions to be asked. At the end of each chapter in part 2, there are lists of such moments for the age group being discussed in that chapter. At the same time, questions will come, and it will most likely be when you are least expecting them. These steps for answering sexuality-related questions have been adapted from the program Real Life, Real Talk (http:// www.reallifereatalk.org/parent-tips/tools.htm), which promotes sexuality education for parents in a variety of cities throughout the United States.

Step #1: Breathe

Taking a moment to focus and reflect on the question, not to mention get your facial expression in-check, sets the tone for the conversation and buys you some time to think.

Step #2: Clarify the Question

Adults understand and treat sexuality issues differently than children do. Where a child might be seeking information or clarification, adults hear the child's desire to try a behavior or fear that the child has been exposed to age-inappropriate concepts. For example, a three-year-old asks, "What does the word *sex* mean?" A clarifying response might be, "Where did you hear that word?" If the child's answer is "My teacher said girls and boys are a different sex," the parent's response will be different than if the child answers "My older sister Jane was talking to her friend on the phone about sex." Clarifying the question allows a parent to learn what a child may already know about the question at hand and focus the response.

Step #3: Provide Accurate and Age-Appropriate Information

When questions are fairly straightforward, the answer may be right at the tip of your tongue. Other questions may require a little research. Either way, using accurate language and keeping messages at an age-appropriate level will help in communicating with your child. If you are unsure what is age-appropriate, check part 2 of this book. Remember, parents make mistakes; information changes. If you provide inaccurate information, admit that you were wrong. This sends a positive message to kids that we all make mistakes and we take responsibility for those mistakes. However, if you don't know the answer, don't lie! Say, "I'll look that up and get back to you," then absolutely follow up.

Step #4: Share Your Values

Information is not enough. Sexuality-related questions give parents an opportunity to share values and faith beliefs with their kids. Combining values with sexuality information shows children that sexuality and faith go together. By addressing issues like intimacy, trust, love, and respect in the context of sexual health questions, parents also keep the focus on healthy sexual development and relationships instead of concentrating on specific sexual behaviors.

Step #5: Follow Up

This step is set on two timetables. Immediately after answering a question, it is a good practice to ask what your child or teen heard and see if they have other questions. They do not need to report verbatim your answer. The purpose of this practice is to make sure that your language wasn't confusing and that you got to the point of their question. It also suggests to a child that you are willing to answer more questions when they have them. In a week, a month, a few days—whatever feels right—pick a teachable moment that gives you the opportunity to refer back to the question. Do this in a way that references but does not result in the same conversation. Then, reinforce the information and values you shared, and again ask if there are further questions.

PART 2

Ages and Stages

Chapter 7

Birth to Kindergarten (0–5)

Laying the Foundation

Parenting Quiz

The response we give our children teaches them how to respond to sexuality issues in their relationships as they grow older. How would you respond to the following statements or scenarios with a toddler, preschooler, or kindergartner? The answers suggested at the end are those that demonstrate comfort with sexuality issues, promote gender equality, build trust through relationship, and show that bodies deserve our care.

1. Mommy, my weenie hurts.
   ___a. I don't want to hear that word in my house. Go tell your father.
   ___b. Remember, we call that a penis, honey. Let's go to the bathroom, look at it, and see what might be wrong.
   ___c. Oh my God! Don't touch it.
   ___d. Can you tell me if something happened? When does it hurt?

2. Ava hugs me too much at school.

___a. Ava loves you. Just be nice and accept the hugs.

___b. Your body belongs to you. You decide who can hug you. Ask for a teacher's help if Ava doesn't listen to your words.

___c. Ava is your friend. Tell her how you feel and remind her to ask before she touches you.

___d. Answer for boy: You're too sensitive; the ladies already love you. Answer for a girl: Girls show emotions by hugging and touching, you'll get used to it.

3. Malcolm has nail polish on, and boys aren't allowed to wear nail polish.

___a. Anyone can wear nail polish. It's a person's choice if they like the color and feel.

___b. You're right. I can't believe his parents let him do that.

___c. Malcolm is a little different from other boys. Just be nice to him.

___d. Boys and girls can do the same things even if they have different bodies. God made us all different. Do you dress and act like all the other boys/girls in your class? (Point out differences between dresses, pants, favorite colors, toys, activities, and so forth.)

4. I'm going to marry my baby sister.

___a. Only boys and girls from different families can get married.

___b. I know you love your sister very much, but she will always be your sister. When we get older we choose to marry someone outside our family so that our family can grow.

___c. No, you can't marry your sister. That's gross.

___d. Being married to someone you love is important. It is a big decision that grown-ups make.

5. Is God a boy?

    __a. It can be hard to picture God because God is not a person like us. So God isn't in a body that is a boy or girl. We can see God in all parts of creation. (Give an example, "When the sun shines in the morning to warm us, we can feel God like a hug.")

    __b. God isn't a boy exactly, but we only say *he* because that's what the Bible says.

    __c. Sometimes we talk about God as *he* or *father*. But God isn't a human boy or man. We also use other names for God like *mother*, *protector*, *spirit*, *love*, *light*, and *friend*.

    __d. God is our leader and strong like boys, so that is why we call God *he* and *father*.

6. Boys have penises, and girls have vaginas.

    __a. You are right. But we don't say those words out loud.

    __b. Yes, a boy's penis and scrotum are on the outside of his body, and a girl's vagina is on the inside. A girl's outside genitals are called a vulva.

    __c. Boys and girls have different private parts, but the rest of their bodies are the same. What other private parts are different on boys and girls? (Here you can make a distinction between inside and outside parts.)

    __d. Shhhh, that's potty talk. Don't talk about girl/boy parts that you don't have, because it's impolite.

Answers: 1: b, d; 2: b, c; 3: a, d; 4: b, d; 5: a, c; 6: b, c

Growing and Changing

The first question that people ask about a pregnancy or a new baby is often related to its sexuality: Is it a boy or a girl? Parents will answer based on genitals seen in an ultrasound or identified just after birth. But the boy or girl label means much more than which box the child will check on forms the rest of his or her life. The label influences how parents, siblings, extended family, teachers, and communities will interact with this child. We help shape a child's gender identity (masculine and feminine) by the name and clothes we choose, the way we talk to the baby, maybe even the way we hold and cuddle the baby. This simple distinction begins crafting a child's sexuality before she or he can even talk or walk.

From birth to age five, learning how to navigate what being identified as a boy or girl means within family, community, and culture is very important. At this age the foundation for sexuality education is cemented. If we wait to talk about health information, relationship etiquette, and family planning conversations until kids are teens, most of the information will be a history lesson. At that point, they already know most of what we waited to tell them; and the values related to the information didn't come from us. Children's sexuality is developing from the moment we name them, hold them, and love them. It is in those moments that education about relationships, bodies, and faith values start. A good foundation in faith and sexuality is integral to helping our children become sexually healthy adults.

Physical Development

Physical development in the birth-to-five age group includes understanding the importance of touch, learning to find and then identify body parts, developing a sense of ownership of one's body, and knowing body part differences and basic reproduction.

The Importance of Touch. An infant's sexuality is shaped by touch, exploration, and relationship. Infants need touch, cuddling, and

bodily warmth to thrive. Many studies have shown that prema-
ture infants who are not touched or held are more likely to fail
to thrive. Infants cannot be spoiled by being held. For the sake of
parents' physical and emotional well-being, we don't hold babies
twenty-four hours a day. Not to mention that babies need to grow
in their independence, too. However, successfully supporting
them as they explore and learn to use their bodies requires safe
and loving hands always there to help if needed.

Boy or Girl or . . .

Not every child is born with easily identifiable male and female
genitalia. These children are called intersex. Intersex is an
umbrella term that relates not only to male and female genitalia. The Intersex Society of North American says, "Intersex is a
general term used for a variety of conditions in which a person
is born with a reproductive or sexual anatomy that doesn't seem
to fit the typical definitions of female or male." This includes
any combination of chromosomes, hormone levels, and internal
and external genitalia. Because there is a wide variety of intersex definitions, it can be difficult to determine the prevalence of
intersex children. "The number comes out to about 1 in 1500 to
1 in 2000 births. But a lot more people than that are born with
subtler forms of sex anatomy variations, some of which won't
show up until later in life."
—Intersex Society of North America, "What Is Intersex?" and "How
Common Is Intersex?" Frequently Asked Questions, http://www
.isna.org/faq/.

At a few months old, babies begin to discover their fingers,
elbows, toes, cheeks, and so on. They also find their genitals. An
adult's reaction to the discovery can model either comfort with
bodies or shame. For example, slapping the baby's hand or pushing it away to put on the diaper sends a message that it is wrong
to touch genitals and they are a bad part of the body. Quick diaper

changes to avoid urination on the changing table can be a necessity. But this is not always the case, and giving infants and babies time without a diaper is good practice for all kinds of issues like diaper rash, early bladder control, and exploring their bodies. Just as a parent might coo and say, "you found your elbow." So, too, should they say, "you found your penis or vulva." Infants also experience erections and vaginal lubrication. In fact, there are ultrasounds of male fetuses with erections. These are natural bodily reactions and should be treated as such. As infants grow to toddlers, parents can teach that bodies respond in certain ways. It is natural and part of how God created us.

Knowledge of Body Parts. Toddlers are curious about all bodies—theirs, their playmates, and grown-ups. Parents can support and nurture curiosity while also teaching privacy and respect. First, naming all the body parts with accurate language helps to avoid messages about genitals as shameful and secret; it also helps to keep children safer from sexual abuse. While playing the body part game we often ask: *Where is your eye? Where is your hand? Show me your knee.* We can add: *point to your penis (or vulva).* Say the words in the exact same inquisitive tone and congratulate your child equally for identifying their foot or their penis/vulva. Accurate language for

Q&A

Child: **Why do you have hair down there?**

Parent: When kids grow up to be adults, their bodies change. Starting when you are a teenager, you will get hair around your penis or vulva, some under your arms, and on your face too. This is one of the ways God created our body to change as we grow up. (If you have a privacy rule that was broken when your child barged in on you and asked the question, you might add: I'm glad I could answer your question. Please remember that in our house, we get privacy to shower and change. Please close the door and go back to what you were playing.)

body parts helps children feel comfortable and knowledgeable talking about their bodies. This way, they can communicate with adults if they need help getting dressed or using the bathroom, and they can also accurately report and describe abuse if it happens.

Toddlerhood can be frustrating. Toddlers desperately want to be independent and "do it themselves," but they still need help with many things: from getting on a chair to opening a package, from using the potty to being fed. Toddlers recognize for the first time that they are their own person, adding "I" to their vocabulary. Privacy, control, and sharing become major lessons. Parents teach about these values as toddlers gain greater control of their bodies and demonstrate good decision making. For example, many children can begin picking out their own clothes and changing with assistance when they are two. Before leaving children to dressing themselves entirely, consider asking them to show you the clothes they pick out so that you can determine if the outfits are weather appropriate and clean, and if they will need help with buttons, ties, and so on. This offers parents an opportunity to explain the reasons or values for prioritizing "rules." For example, weather

Q&A

Parent: "Give Aunt Maria a hug good-bye"
Child: Hiding behind your legs, shakes head no and doesn't speak.

Relatives can often be hurt when a child does not want to kiss or hug them. Forcing a child to kiss or hug another person sends a mixed message about consenting to unwanted touch. A parent in this situation may say, "You get to make choices about your body and who touches it. We don't need to do a hug. But it is impolite to not say good-bye." Reach down and comfortably hold the child so they turn to the relative and assist them in waving or shaking hands if the child will cooperate. As a parent, if you are clear about your value of owning one's body and touching without permission only when safety or cleanliness are at issue, relatives will understand.

appropriate and clean clothes are ways to keep our bodies safe and show that we care about the gift that God gave us.

Allowing others to help us is part of forming good relationships; it doesn't mean a child is weak or a "baby." It shows that they are smart and resourceful. Remember, asking for help with clothes lasts our entire lives—think about cuff links and fancy dress zippers. Parents can start slowly with jointly picking clothes, laying them out so that they are easier to put on, and sharing tricks like sitting down to get both legs into pants. Eventually, as toddlers are able to dress themselves and make good decisions about clothing, they can be given more and more privacy. The same learning style is true about bathing and potty training. Teach some basic values, like God created us so we show our thanks by keeping ourselves clean. Provide hands-on training on the how-tos of washing. Give smaller tasks first like brushing teeth, washing hands, wiping after urinating, and then build up to bigger tasks like brushing hair, washing the whole body, and rinsing out shampoo. Skills and values shared that relate to bathing, dressing, and potty training lay the foundation for a variety of sexuality-related messages about control, privacy, and sharing as related to bodies.

Ownership of one's body. Around preschool, and certainly in kindergarten, children become conscious about their own body, how it appears to others, and how it functions. In many childcare and early schooling settings, bathrooms are open and gender neutral. Kids see each other's bodies with some regularity. They may also be curious about each other's bodies, touching or playing doctor. When children are within a year of each other and in the same playgroup or classroom, it is typical for their curiosity to find an imaginative play outlet. Young children engage in this play as *researchers*, not with an intent to harm or express sexual desire as our *adult glasses* might suggest. In fact, comfort with nudity teaches a strong message about body image acceptance and love of self.

Of course, a simultaneous message about privacy needs to be taught. If you find children playing doctor while naked or inspecting each other's genitals you might say:

God created our bodies and they are good. But they also belong to us. We are not allowed to touch other people's genitals without permission or unless a person needs our help (like doctors and parents help children). Our genitals, vulva, and penis are private. They are a special part of our body, and other children should not touch them.

At that point, a parent may also choose to include a message about self-touching or save that for another time. For example, you might say, "Touching our private parts can feel good. You can touch yourself when you are alone in a private room. Can you tell me a private place (bedroom, bathroom)?" These responses affirm our bodies, pleasure, and touch as positive and also place limits on age-appropriate types of touching and name acceptable places.

Playing doctor or touching and showing genitals in this young age group is common. It is common through elementary school, in fact. Responding to this natural curiosity in a calm manner is important. Even though this behavior is common, there can be times when it is not appropriate. The children involved should not be more than one or two years apart in age or abilities. They should know each other fairly well. The play should not involve force or illicit strong emotions like anger. In other words, this play should be recognizable as familiar, everyday, healthy ways our kids explore their worlds.[1]

Basic Reproduction Information. Four- and five-year-old kids' curiosity about bodies often includes questions about where babies come from. Their literal orientation to the world really means that they want to know: where is the physical location of the baby and how does it get out? Teaching accurate language for body parts for both boys and girls lays the foundation for discussing where babies come from and how they are made in a factual and natural manner. There are a few progressively informative ways to answer the question, Where do babies come from? The answer you give depends on how much your child already knows about anatomy and the context of the question.

For example, a child might look at a pregnant woman or mother and ask, How does the baby come out? Remember the steps to answering children's questions (see pages 31–33) and clarify the question if needed. In this scenario, the specific question can be answered with something like, "The baby is growing in a place in her body called the uterus, not her stomach. The uterus is connected to her vagina, a tube that leads to an opening between her legs. When the baby is ready, it will come out of her vagina." Presumably your child already knows these two parts of female anatomy, if not, you may want to bring up a picture or open a book such as It's NOT the Stork.

There are exceptions to the typical birth and conception lesson. If the baby being discussed will be born through cesarean section, you can add, "But this baby will be born differently because the doctor needs to help the Mommy. They will make a cut through her skin and open the uterus." Generally a cut-open abdomen and c-section is "grosser" to a child than describing vaginal birth. And in all cases, "cutting the tummy or stomach open" is incorrect anatomy.

Other children may be "made" or conceived using assisted reproductive technologies (ARTs). There are age-appropriate books to help explain surrogacy, in vitro fertilization, and artificial insemination, depending on the particular circumstances of birth. ARTparenting.org is a great resource for parents developed by the

Q&A

Child: **When can people have babies?**

Parent: Our bodies need to change to be more like a grown-up before we can have babies. These changes are called puberty and happen mostly during high school. Even if our bodies can have babies, we believe that God wants us to take special care of babies. That means most people wait to have a baby until they can make grown-up decisions and provide for a child like having a job and money to pay for things a baby needs.

Harvard Medical School Center for Mental Health and Media. The site shares personal stories, resources, and conversation starters. No matter the circumstances, the lesson of vaginal birth is important for children's overall knowledge of reproduction.

The basic steps of reproduction may be easier to share than a definition of intercourse. "When grown-ups love each other, they like to kiss and hug and touch each other in ways that feel good. Sometimes, a man and a woman place the man's penis into the woman's vagina. The man's penis releases sperm into the woman, which can meet her egg in the uterus, and sometimes a baby begins."

Most children will respond by saying, "Ewww, I'm so glad that's only for grown-ups"; "Gross"; or "I'll never do that." The genius of this response is its simplicity, while still naming a profound connection between love, pleasure, and reproduction. In *From Diapers to Dating*, Debra W. Haffner shares more detailed approaches to explaining intercourse to a child between 5–8 years old. Based on your values, you may want to change the relationship situation. For those who have used assisted reproductive technology, there are other resources available to explain to young children how they or their friends were made (see page 45).

—Debra W. Haffner, *From Diapers to Dating: A Parent's Guide to Raising Sexually Healthy Children* (New York: New Market Press, 2000), 98.

"How did it get there?" might be a follow-up question, or the question might have started out broadly like, "How are babies made?" By the time a child is five, they can understand the following information about reproduction:

+ A sperm from a man and an ovum/egg from a woman meet in a woman's body to make a baby.
+ The sperm gets into a woman's body from a man's penis.
+ The baby grows in the uterus and comes out the vagina.

There may be many different ways and times you share this information. Parents may build on it when questions arise or get a book to share if the question is never asked. By five, kids have their own theories. Without a parent explaining the reproductive process, children may be very confused. Not to mention, they will learn this isn't a subject adults talk about. Parents can lose their credibility and comfort level in the eyes of their children as a source of sexuality information.

Relational Development

Relational development in the birth-to-five age group includes developing trust, modeling affection and expression of feelings, and promoting gender equity.

Developing Trust. Questions related to reproduction inevitably overlap physical development and relational development issues. Children ask questions of their parents because they are curious but also because they trust them as a source of information. Trust is built in the everyday moments of parenting. Creating a caring environment where children feel safe and loved and have basic needs met nurtures trust. Trust is also built when parents provide learning opportunities such as waiting for a turn, following through on a promise, creating jobs for small children to contribute to the family as a whole, and applying family rules and consequences consistently and justly.

From a relational perspective, once children can identify *themselves* as an individual, they learn to respect *others* as individuals. Respect for others (the first step to love of neighbor) is taught through lessons of sharing and valuing others. For example, toddlers and preschoolers go through a process of learning about personal space. Sometimes children are interested in a mother's breasts, crawl under a skirt, or hide in between pant legs. This behavior may also carry over to friends whom they hug too exuberantly or kiss even when met with protest. Young children have a different sense of personal space, to say the least. Teaching respect for others means controlling our bodily impulses, showing affection in a variety of ways, and sharing feelings without harming or disrespecting others (all good lessons for later in life).

Developing trust in and respect for others also means we are in multiple relationships at the same time. Young children often want to be the sole focus of parental attention and love. The parent-child relationship is challenged by other siblings' presence, developing friendships, and even by the parents' romantic relationship with each other. By naming these situations openly, children learn that parents can love many people at the same time. For example, "I love you very much. But I also love mommy and your sister/brother. I have enough love for all of you, just like God has enough love for all of us." This lesson relates to the love commandment, which calls us to have balance among God, self, and other in all our relationships.

Preschoolers often face the issue of balancing relationships rather abruptly when a new child is welcomed into the family or a friend decides to play with someone else today—"But Eli cannot be her friend, he is my friend." Parents and teachers are the guides in these situations by responding that Eli can be friends with more than one person by making time to play with people at different times.

Q&A

Child: **What does married mean?**

Parent: Being married is when two people decide that they love each other and want to be together for a long time. They promise to make decisions together and care for each other. Sometimes married people decide to make their family bigger by having kids or taking care of kids who need a home.

Expressing Emotions. How well or comfortable we are sharing our emotions is another important aspect of communication in relationships. Preschool and kindergartners tend to know three feelings: happy, sad, and mad. There is a wide spectrum of emotion that many of us never learn to use in order to communicate more specifically how we feel. Expanding a young child's vocabulary to include frustrated, confused, excited, and lonely begins to put more specific characteristics to interactions children have. For example, if a child is starting a new school, "sad" doesn't fully describe their feelings as well as a mix of excited, confused, and lonely or nervous might. Parents who name a variety of feelings in their own experience but also who help their child reflect on experiences begin to provide broader and more specific ways for a child to communicate in relationships.

Indirectly, children learn from how grown-ups around them show and share emotion. Grown men are less likely to model sharing feelings like hugging and kissing or saying "I love you" to boy children. Boy children are often taught not to share emotions when told "boys don't cry" and "be a big boy." Unfortunately, these instances are often related to sharing emotion and communication skills. Similarly, girls are coddled and referred to as sensitive or "a real drama queen." Mothers are often faulted for being too emotional with their sons and damaging their masculinity (which is not possible). These seemingly minor social cues can set us up for a lifetime of miscommunication and assumptions about how we should establish intimacy.

Gender Equity. How parents communicate will partially determine whether their children take on gendered stereotypes or learn skills to express how they feel, regardless of gender. In fact, temperament and personality probably influence a child's level of emotionality more than gender or sex. Gender inequality has no place in the expression of our feelings or affection. From a young age, all children should be encouraged to name their feelings, respond according to those feelings without harming others, and be able to listen to others express their feelings. This provides a strong foundation for healthy relationships in all aspects of life.

Sex and gender inform who we are; they do not determine it. Learning to navigate what society expects of gender is different from requiring compliance with it. At an early age, some parents limit children's interests and creativity by allowing sex and gender to determine the clothes they can wear or the activities they do. Comments about what girls should do and what boys should do have lasting, often negative, effects on children's self-identity.

> **Q&A**
>
> *Child:* Derek says, "Boys aren't supposed to cry; he called me a baby."
>
> *Parent:* You are not a baby. Everyone cries. It is our body's way of showing people that we are sad. Crying helps us share those feelings. God wants us to be able to share our feelings—sad, angry, happy, excited—because it makes us feel better and helps people around us understand us better.

The enforcement of gender roles is often at its peak in preschool and kindergarten years. Some sociologists suspect this is true because the world functions on assigned gender roles that children are trying to understand and assimilate. In other words, they are trying to be "like adults." Further, telling children that gender doesn't matter and that they can do whatever they please is a very confusing statement to a child (if not a lie).

Gender does matter. There is still great inequality in our world based on the sex and gender of people. Between three and five years old, children recognize traditional male and female gender roles and often reinforce them in their play. Young children begin to have a sense of their own sex (male, female, and intersex) and the ability to recognize other people's sex based on gender characteristics. The ability to identify sex and gender is a developmental task. Children, however, can understand that one's sex (male or female) does not absolutely mean a person will like specific girl or boy things. In fact, children need to learn how to negotiate cultural understandings of gender if any generation is to become successful at achieving gender equity.

Children learn that differences exist across genders quite readily. The question is do grown-ups reinforce the gender stereotypes or do they support gender equity. Here are examples of teaching opportunities for affirming gender equality—affirm when boys cry, girls wear pants, boys wear nail polish, women have different types of jobs, men drop-off/pick-up children, girls play sports, or boys engage in "homemaking" imaginary play. Diversity of gendered behavior will teach children that there is a link (albeit fuzzy) between sex and gender, but also that there is a wide range of expression and overlap among genders and sexes.

Babies, toddlers, and early school children are observant and astute. They watch us, learn from us, are confused by us, and are shaped by us. Parents who model communication skills, including sharing feelings in a gender-equitable way, help children on a path toward healthy relationships and a positive self-image.

Faith Development

Infants to kindergartners experience faith through other people. This does not mean that they do not have their own faith or belief, but that they learn faith through relationships with others, like parents and caregivers. Learning about religion or being faithful is different from being a good person. Hopefully those things are related to one another, but new research suggests that babies might have a moral sense of right and wrong very early. Researchers Paul Bloom and Karen Wynn at Yale University discuss findings on babies' "naive moral" sense.[2] Through cleaver and well-designed experiments using looking time (how long a child maintains visual attention) for infants and responses to need or distress from mobile babies, researchers discovered that babies have a general and rudimentary sense of compassion and empathy. These characteristics are a starting point for morality. Babies can determine, to greater and lesser extents, what matters—responding to distress and preference of individuals who help—as well as respond with like and dislike to adult moral behaviors. For example, given two puppet scenarios where one puppet shares or helps and the other hinders, babies tend to grab the helping puppet, indicating a preference for "helpers" and an aversion to "hinderers."

What are parents to do with this naive moral sense and how does it relate to faith development? This research suggests that infants may have the foundational capacity to tell the difference between right and wrong in common moral situations. Babies need grown-ups to work with them to build on that capacity because simple right and wrong situations become more complex as we get older, not to mention that some aspects of morality are shaped by communities and differ across cultures. As noted earlier, children are most likely to act the same way that they see adults and role models acting in their lives. Leading by example is one way to encourage decision making based on faith values. But parents should also take opportunities to talk about decision making and values with young children to make sure that they understand the connection. For example, your family might donate food or service to people in need. What decisions do you make about which organizations to work with, or how to best help, or how much time you will contribute? What faith values are the foundation for these decisions? Talking, even with young children, about these choices helps them nurture a sense of connection between faith values and life decisions.

Q&A

Child: **Does God love everyone the same?**

Parent: God loves everyone and every part of creation. I think God loves people in a way that helps them best. People might feel that love differently because we are all unique parts of God's creation. But that doesn't mean God loves any person more or less than another.

Similarly, babies and toddlers learn faith concepts like trust, faith, and love through objects and relationships that have relevance to them.[3] For example, a blankie might be as important to a child as the cross or Communion may become to an adult.

Treating such objects with care and nurturing a sense of ritual meaning for them can translate into similar faith practices later in a child's life. This is not to say that blankies, pacifiers, or stuffed animals should stay around forever. They are, as child psychologists would call them, transitional objects. Rather, the practice of using objects to evoke a safe feeling, of ritualizing a bedtime routine, or of learning to "talk" and give life to a stuffed animal (symbol) will be similar to sacramental practices, rituals of liturgy, and prayer. Honoring young children's connection to these objects and rituals is an important step in their faith development.

For many young children, their parents are their first model of God. God as mother and father makes sense to young children. Parents show love, care for basic needs, and are seemingly ever present. They are also the ones who discipline, help, and teach. There can be a downside to the association children make between parents and God. Parents are not perfect, and in cases of abuse, neglect, or distant emotional connection, a young child's relationship with God can suffer. Worship spaces and Sunday schools can share a variety of the images of God, as mother and father; as environmental images (sun, light, water); and as feelings or actions (love, care, protection). Such language for God is a starting point for deep spiritual connection as well as positive affirmations of gender. This also means that parents can positively role model different gendered aspects of how God might be understood. Religious images and language matter when we are children, and we carry it with us as adults.

The parent as a model for God and transitional objects that teach ritual are two implicit parenting practices that contribute to faith development. There may be times as children grow older where parents start to draw connections between the two. Parents may point out that the parent is not perfect, like God is perfect. As a parent you talk to God in prayer like your child talks to their favorite stuffed animal. It is equally important to begin sharing Scripture and congregational practices so that children learn about their faith family. From two to five years old, children will take Scripture stories as true, literal events that have happened. They will continue to do this even into elementary school. Specific stories like images of Jesus in heaven, battles, or miracle cures of tormented people can lead to negative fantasies or associating religion with scary events. There is good reason Sunday school curriculum at this age focuses on stories about creation, Noah's ark, successes of matriarchs and patriarchs in the Hebrew Scriptures, Jesus' childhood, and feel-good miracles, including the Easter rising. Faith stories are like family histories, most of us wait until kids are a little older to share the tragedies and we err on the side of happy endings.

What babies' moral sense is or is not has yet to be fully understood. Nonetheless, parents have an integral role to play in the moral and faith development of their children beginning at a young age. Religious messages for this age should always be: "God and Jesus love you. We show that love to yourself and other people by helping, caring, and sharing." That message is a primary Christian value. It is also a foundational sexuality education lesson. Healthy relationships reflect a love of self and other, through God's presence. The earlier children learn this, the easier it is for them to identify these qualities in their relationships and apply these values to decision making.

Connecting Faith and Sexuality Education

Babies, toddlers, preschoolers, and kindergartners are learning about relationships and most often do this through their bodies—through increasing movement, touching, and playing. This is possibly the most sensuous stage of human development because of the connection to and use of our bodies to feel and discover the world. Faith practices often support this way of learning and knowing God, which nurtures young children's sexuality and positive body image.

In traditions that baptize infants, a child experiences blessing and membership through a sensory experience including being held by family in the sanctuary, passed and securely held by a clergy person, then anointed with water that has particular smells and sounds associated with it. This is not a sexual event, but intimacy and sensuality are part of the experience, and the relationship of love within the family is broadened to include a congregational community. Not to mention, baptisms are teachable moments to talk about reproduction and choices that go into having or not having children. As a parent, you might invite a conversation about how much time, effort, and love go into raising a child and maybe even comment about how you made decisions about when or how to expand your family. This is also a time to talk about why it's important to have a community to help raise children, like the congregation. Baptisms also demonstrate what family structures a congregation publicly supports.

Young children benefit from being in worship, even if it is only from time to time or a small amount every Sunday. Some congregations have childcare during the full service for this age group. It's understandable that some parents need a break on Sunday morning and want to experience church free of cries, constant questions, or snacking distractions. However, in worship, young children can experience similar affirmations of intimacy and sensuality to the baptismal experience described above. Showing affection to children during worship—sitting close, hugging, kissing, and holding them—sends a message that parents, the faith community, and God support loving, physical forms of affection. Additionally, the simple decision to wear nice clothes to church on a regular basis instills a practice of care for our bodies and thankfulness to God. However, if the clothes are uncomfortable, stuffy, and restrictive, the care for body message may be replaced by a notion that our bodies need to be hidden and confined to be proper.

Parents often feel pressured to keep their children quiet and out of sight in worship services. Congregations who do not support children's presence in worship (even for a short time) are doing a disservice to their youngest members.[4] Worship can be a time to share faith practices with and educate children. Instead of lots of shh's, worship can contribute to faith development when parents and educators

+ make it about enjoying time together and celebrating community;

+ focus on leading children through greetings, prayers, singing, and lessons;
+ occasionally note why the congregation does things a certain way.

For example, if the congregation uses responsive prayer, babies and toddlers see parents take a moment to join in that prayer and recognize the whole congregation talking at the same time. From four and five, parents can point out words that the child knows in that prayer and invite children to join in as they are able. A parent might say:

We read a prayer together to involve everyone in worship. It isn't just the minister who talks. And it reminds us of what we should be thinking about when we come to church. It also means we work together as a congregation to talk at the same time.

Inclusivity, community, and putting God first through prayer in our worship are values children will learn to identify if they are pointed out. Parents might also choose to point out specific language, such as names for God that would teach about gender equity or God's presence in the environment. We might also use prayers at home over a meal or before bed that use a variety of images of God if our faith community does not.

In addition to worship, Sunday school has specific tasks related to sexuality education. Young children learn from children's book characters just as they learn from biblical stories: how to imagine new worlds, navigate a difficult situation, or act in social settings. There are age-appropriate sexuality messages in biblical stories for preschool and kindergarten ages. The story of creation teaches young children that they are special because they are created by God. This lesson should be connected to education about caring for bodies and respecting others' bodies. Sunday school teachers should be reminded to use accurate language for body parts in helping with the bathroom or reminding children about privacy issues in the classroom. Noah's ark is a perfect moment to discuss reproduction. Some children may know why Noah brought two of every animal on the ark and others may not. The teacher can simply ask the class if they know and then state, "Yes, most animals need to have a male and female to make a baby. Noah wanted the animals to have babies after the Ark landed safely again." *Most* is a key word in that phrase. Inevitably one child will share that worms don't need a male and female! Using "most" also honors families who have used assisted reproductive technologies and sticks to the facts of reproduction instead of these animals creating families with a mom and dad—which is not an accurate representation of most animal mating.

Stories about Joseph (Gen. 37:1–28), Miriam (Exod. 2:1–10), and David (1 Sam. 16) reinforce that children are a special part of God's plan and that at each stage of life we have unique gifts to share. The Gospel stories provide a platform for lessons on neighbor love (Mark 12:31; John 15:12), respect for the least among us (Matt. 5:1–12), helping each other (Luke 10:25–37), and sharing the story of Jesus and God (Matt. 25:14–30; Acts 16:16–34). These stories are examples of how to act and what values like justice, respect, love, and compassion look like in practice. In order to help children make the connection between a story and their actions, parents and religious education programs need to connect these stories to age-appropriate examples. Sharing snacks in a classroom, in our homes, or at the playground is like making loaves and fish for the 5,000 (Mark 6:30–44). Collecting coins, food, or clothes for families and children without these things is like the woman who gives her two coins (Luke 21:1–4) or when Jesus heals sick people (Matt. 15:21–28; Mark 1:40–45; Luke 13:10–17). Being created by God means that we need to respect each other and may not touch each other without permission, and that touch needs to be loving and helpful not hurtful (punching, pushing, pinching). Learning the values of the faith tradition in caring relationships at home and in the congregation serves as the foundation for healthy sexual and moral development. In the moment when a preschooler belts out the tune "Jesus Loves Me" or "This Little Light of Mine," it is evident that they feel it in a way that brings faith practice and sexuality together in a celebration of God's affirmation of them as unique and loved.

TEACHABLE MESSAGES AND MOMENTS

God created our bodies, and they are good.

+ Name body parts accurately and teach about internal and external genitalia.
+ Reinforce respect and care for the body and other's bodies.
+ Encourage increased independence and responsibility for body with bathing, dressing, and potty training.
+ Assure that touching of the penis or vulva is okay and can be done in a private space.
+ Tell how reproduction happens and the location a baby grows and is birthed from.

Relationships are based on faith values of love, respect, equality, and shared responsibility.

+ Discuss how families choose to have babies or not.
+ Point out family practices or rules that show values of respect, love and sharing.
+ Do not force gendered play or identification and assess parental examples of and response to gendered behavior.
+ Remember that the parental relationship is the first model for "godly love" and "romantic love." Talk about which adults are allowed to touch their body and in what ways (parents, doctors, and teachers, childcare providers if help is needed in the bathroom). Prepare them to say no to an adult who tries to touch their genitals or make them touch theirs and tell a trusted adult if something does happen.

REFLECTIONS

Write down a few things you learned from this chapter, some examples from your own life that reflect the teachable messages, or a reminder of something you want to do or say.

Chapter 8

Elementary School Years (6–10)

Gathering Information

Parenting Quiz

Elementary school kids are faced with a rapidly expanding world and need their parents to be active participants in helping them understand it. Kids begin to find other sources for information and have an expanding number of adults to whom they can ask questions. Yet parents remain the primary sexuality educator throughout a child's life. The answers suggested at the end are those that demonstrate comfort with sexuality issues, promote gender equality, build trust through relationship, and show that bodies deserve our care. How might you respond to the following statements or scenarios with elementary school children?

1. Mom, get out of the bathroom! I need privacy in the shower and getting dressed.

   ___a. Yes, of course you can have your privacy. However, you need to show that you can wash your hair and body, and clean up after yourself too. I'll be back to check.

___b. No, silly. You are my little baby; let me help.

___c. Sure, let me know if you need my help. I'm glad you want to take responsibility for caring for your body.

___d. Don't be a prude. Everyone in this house shares a bathroom, and you have nothing to see anyway.

2. Mom, why do the boys always pretend the girls have cooties? I like playing with the girls.

___a. Boys need to play boy things. You shouldn't be playing with the girls.

___b. Which one do you like? I remember this one boy in my class who always played with the girls and tried to kiss us.

___c. Everyone has different interests. God created each of us to be unique. I hope you find friends based on what you like to do and not based on whether they are a boy or girl.

___d. At this age, some boys find it difficult to share what they think and feel with girls. Saying girls have cooties or teasing them is a way to get girls' attention. It can be hurtful to girls to say they are "bad" or different. I hope you are a good friend to boys and girls.

3. I can't find a shirt to wear because my chest looks funny with these things growing.

___a. Those things are called breast buds, and it means that you are starting puberty. Our bodies are made to change and grow. You're ready to wear tank top undershirts.

___b. Just find something to wear. You're not even close to big enough to complain.

___c. Looks like someone is growing up. Just wait until you get big boobs and have to wear a bra every day.

___d. Your body is changing, and it can be uncomfortable sometimes. Let me help you find a shirt that feels right.

4. Michael has been my best friend since kindergarten. He never plays with me anymore because I don't want to play baseball at recess.

___a. There are other kids in school. Find a new friend.

___b. It can be frustrating when our friends find new interests or new friends. I know you must miss Michael. Did you tell him you miss playing with him?

___c. You have some new friends too this year. I wonder if Michael feels the same way. Why don't you invite him over after school and see if you can find something to do together here?

___d. Friends come and go. Michael will outgrow his baseball obsession. Just give him time.

5. Why do the boyfriends and girlfriends on the show always kiss?

___a. Kissing is one way to show that they like each other. Romantic kissing is different from when I kiss you. Both are saying, "I love/like you" in a special way.

___b. Two people kiss in a romantic way because it feels good. People should kiss only after they have known each other for a long time and call each other boyfriend/girlfriend. Kids who are in middle school do this sometimes. (Add in your family value related to age.)

___c. That's a TV show. It isn't real. You'll kiss someone like that when you marry them.

___d. They have to kiss because they are at the end of their date and they're supposed to do that.

6. The second grade teacher left school because she had her baby. I'm not going to have any babies and miss school.

___a. Lots of people don't plan to have babies. We just welcome them as gifts.

___b. Grown-ups can do their best to plan when to have a baby, but not the exact day. The school will find a teacher to take her place until she decides when to come back and teach.

__c. Babies are a great blessing. You can plan to have a baby or not (with your partner). But, I'm glad you plan to finish all your schooling before you make that decision. The teacher is not a student anymore. Teaching is her job, and she can take time off to have a baby.

__d. Babies come when they want. The teacher will be back in no time.

7. I don't like those clothes. I want this style instead. It's what the older kids wear.

__a. When you are older, we can discuss whether or not you can wear those clothes. Right now, you need to buy clothes for your age in this section.

__b. OK, let's try it on. I never got to have cool clothes when I was a kid and really hated that.

__c. You're a little kid. You can't wear big kid clothes like that. You'll look silly.

__d. I understand why you like those clothes, but they aren't appropriate for your age. How we dress is a way of telling people that we care about our bodies and like who we are as we are.

Answers: 1: a, c; 2: c, d; 3: a, d; 4: b, c; 5: a, b; 6: b, c; 7: a, d

Growing and Changing

Six- to ten-year-olds have to sift through many new experiences with rapidly increasing independence at school, clubs, and sports and with a widening group of peers. The elementary school years are often labeled latent, meaning dormant, resting, waiting for suitable conditions for growth or maturation. Nothing could be further from the truth. In elementary school, kids' bodies, relationships, and faith are changing in significant ways. They are like active sponges, soaking up important information, practicing at relationships, and learning to navigate a more adult world. The best thing is: elementary kids openly want their parents to be part of their lives and decisions.

Physical Development

Six-year-olds have lost their baby body and looks for the most part. They have often thinned out, grown taller, and are in better control of their movements. Running, jumping, climbing monkey bars, pumping a swing, and riding a bike are some of the new ways they practice their coordination and strength. Children continue to hone these skills along with reading, writing, math, and science as they move through elementary school. A child's feeling of comfort and confidence with her body grows as she gains physical control and conquers feats once considered impossible. This goes hand-in-hand with recognizing differences in other people's bodies. Some children are faster runners, have very neat handwriting, are good at playing the piano, or are able to throw a baseball or kick a soccer ball. Parents need to help children understand that physical differences are part of God's unique creation. A positive body image begins with accepting what each of us was uniquely given by God and seeing how it complements others. Unfortunately, this is not the message kids often get from media or their peers. Positive comments about elementary school-age children's dress, body type, and physical ability are important keys to developing a positive body image through the teenage years.

In elementary school, kids usually become shy about their bodies and may want privacy when dressing and bathing. The timing and intensity of wanting privacy may depend on how nudity is handled in the household. Some homes have open-door policies where bathrooms are available for use by multiple people at the same time, regardless of sex. Others may practice dividing bathrooms and dressing by sex. Moms and daughters or dads and sons are fine to use the bathroom or dress together. Or, the household may have a strict one person at a time rule. Either way, being consistent with household rules and explaining why they exist is important to sharing your values on privacy and nudity. When a child desires increased privacy, parents can encourage him to take responsibility for his body and use the opportunity as a teachable moment on privacy and values about nudity.

Q&A

Child: **Moooom! You can't come in here right now!**

Parent: Step out of the room and keep the door cracked. "I didn't mean to interrupt your privacy. But you need to remember to wash out all the shampoo. Do you want help with that quickly, and then I can leave again?"

Similar to toddlers and preschoolers, elementary-age children take increasing responsibility for their dress, bathing, and hygiene. Given their age, elementary kids have the capacity to do this. Parents do not need to finish the hair washing, check the teeth, or towel drying after a bath. Of course, like all parenting changes this is gradual and children need to demonstrate that they are taking responsibility before everything is turned over to them. By six, children should be getting themselves dressed and choosing appropriate clothing for the weather and the occasion. As they move through elementary school, parents can encourage kids to hone their style as it reflects their unique personality and honors the body God gave them. This may mean that they match crazy colors together but choose clothes that are clean and in season. Parents can help elementary-age kids successfully take responsibility for their bodies by starting a routine for bathing, dressing, hair washing, and tooth care. This way parents can concentrate on reminding a child about the routine instead of nagging about the finer points of drying off after a shower or cleaning under every nail. Not every child will be at the same place with these tasks, but encouraging and supporting a child in first grade can lead to an independent and responsible ten-year-old.

Changes in privacy and taking responsibility for one's body are also great opportunities to talk about values related to nudity. The value that our bodies are good because God created them has come up a number of times already. For elementary age children, it can be confusing to say that our bodies are great, yet nudity requires privacy especially as we get older. It suggests something magical has changed and perhaps for the worse. The days of running out of the bathroom naked and being chased by a parent with a towel are gone. Is there some secret kid code that tells them this isn't OK anymore? Actually, it isn't so secret, and they know that. Some kids observe grown-ups becoming visibly uncomfortable with such behavior or have been directly told to change. Parents who begin giving their child responsibility for certain bathing and dressing tasks in toddlerhood may have an easier time now talking with her about doing most of this for herself. A parent might find opportunities to convey the following message about privacy and nudity:

> God made our bodies, and they are good. We take care of them because they are such a special gift. Each of us, as we grow older, learns to do that on our own. Privacy is one way that we take the time we need to care for our body and keep our body safe.

This statement teaches the value that bodies are good and that privacy increases with responsible care for our bodies. It also supports a message of safety related to privacy.

In this age group, kids may begin to explore their bodies out of curiosity and pleasure. In teaching the term *masturbation* for this behavior, parents can reinforce messages from the younger years that people touch themselves to learn about their bodies, it can be pleasurable, but it is something done in private. Masturbation may in fact empower children to learn about their bodies and know how to keep themselves safe. It is not addictive, nor does it have any relationship to your child's likelihood to engage in sexual behaviors at this age. In the teen years, I address how promotion of masturbation and other outercourse (nonpenetrative) behaviors may reduce their likelihood to engage in forms of intercourse (see pages 129-30). At this elementary age, the behavior labeled masturbation is not usually genital touching with the intent to orgasm. In many cases, kids are just exploring the parts they have and how their body responds.

During the elementary years, parents and educators need to provide children with clear and specific sexual abuse prevention information. Parents and educators (because sometimes the parent is the abuser) need to help children identify what kind of help with physical tasks is appropriate and when touching of a child's body, especially the genitals, is permissible. For example, a doctor's exam or helping if there is a particularly messy bowel movement may be the only times a child's genitals need to be touched or inspected. Knowing the context of appropriate touch versus inappropriate touch is one aspect of sexual abuse prevention.

Q&A

What do I do if my child tells me someone touched them inappropriately or sexually abused them?

Start by affirming your child, "You were very brave to tell me what happened." Take some quick notes on what your child told you so you don't mix up information in your head. Depending on the severity of the abuse or harassment, check on the facts of the situation and the parties involved. Report the abuse or help your child report the abuse to the correct authority figure—youth group leader, pastor, principal, teacher, coach, or police.

Our culture usually paints a picture of a creepy guy in the park as the likely child abuser, yet this is least often the case. Most children are abused by someone they know and trust—a babysitter, coach, teacher, family member, and so on. Children need to be told that "no matter who" touches or asks to be touched by them, it is wrong—even if the child knows and loves the abuser. Kids who hear that "it is grown-ups' responsibility to keep kids safe, and it is never a child's fault" will have a counter voice from an abuser who tries to shame a child into thinking that the abuse is something special or, alternatively, part of a punishment. Honest and informative conversation with elementary school-age children keeps them safer. It can be done in a way that does not scare them, but prepares them for what may happen in their lives. Here are sexual abuse prevention messages to share with your child:

+ Identify with your child what types of behavior constitute sexual abuse.
+ Reinforce the message that our bodies belong to us and others should not touch us without permission, especially our genitals.
+ Encourage the child to find a trusted adult immediately if someone does touch the child's genitals or asks the child to touch the grown-up's genitals.
+ Help them list a few trusted adults whom they could tell. Since abuse can happen anywhere, make sure that these are people in different arenas of your child's life (family, school, church, and so forth).

Elementary-age kids thrive on learning new things, from new subjects in school to the latest hit cartoons and music. Sexual abuse prevention is part of the information that they need as they grow older. They also need to begin learning about puberty and how babies are made (meaning, intercourse) if they have not already. This age group tends to ask very factual questions. They may enjoy books and pamphlets with pictures to help them understand the information. Some parents may feel that elementary school is too early to start teaching about puberty and intercourse. Consider these two facts:

1. Kids at this age learn from other kids and the media (TV, music, and the Internet). Proactive parents have a chance to share the information first and explain their values.
2. Being prepared for puberty helps kids to be more comfortable and less anxious about changes, as well as more open and less afraid about their sexuality-related questions.

By nine or ten, kids may begin to experience early signs of puberty. Girls start to display signs of changing secondary-sex characteristics—oily skin, increased sweating, breast buds, and hair growth under arms and on genital areas—on average earlier than boys. Girls may also experience a growth spurt, getting significantly taller and gaining weight. This begins, on average, closer

Q&A

Girl: **There is blood in my underwear. What's wrong?**

Parent: "I'm glad you came to tell me what happened. You are probably fine. Please go to the bathroom and dab toilet paper on your vulva to check if you are still bleeding." It could be a few things: a larger cut, her hymen breaking, or her period. A larger cut you would handle just like any other accident, making sure to find out how it happened. If it was just a spot and probably her hymen, you might say, "Around your age, many girls break their hymen from doing physical activity. Your hymen is a small thin piece of skin just inside your vagina. Maybe you were running, jumping, or biking today. It will heal on its own, and you won't even know it happened." (If your daughter has started her period, the blood will not be a consistent stream and there will be discoloration and other fluids. See page 92 for a discussion of menstruation.)

to age ten or eleven in boys. Some girls get their first period, or menarche, at nine years old, but the average is still closer to twelve years old in the United States. Menarche and spermenarche—the first ejaculation with live sperm in it—are not the markers of puberty. They are the point at which a boy's body is creating sperm and a girl's body starts releasing an egg. They are part of puberty, but there are many changes happening that will occur before and after those events in a child's life. Preparing kids for these changes means giving them information prior to puberty starting and then supporting them throughout the time.

Physical changes are not the only aspect of sexuality education that six- to ten-year-olds need. They can now understand in a fuller sense how a baby is made, why and how people choose to have or not have babies, and how intercourse is for more than just making babies. Beginning in first grade, a parent can find opportunities to explain the internal and external genitalia of women and men. As the child ages, a parent can build on this information and describe changes that will come with puberty. Interspersing a sexuality education book into a weekly reading routine is a great way to bring up questions and share information without sexuality seeming out of place from other learning experiences. Once children have a renewed understanding of male and female genitalia and the new knowledge that ovaries make eggs and testicles make sperm, the stage is set for learning "how a baby is made." A parent may say something like:

> Sometimes when a man and woman love each other they share private time together where they kiss and touch each other. This feels good. A man's penis can become hard or erect and a woman's vagina can become wet or lubricated. They can put the man's penis inside the woman's vagina and sperm come out that can meet up with the egg traveling into the woman's uterus. We call this intercourse, and sometimes it leads to having a baby.

This message gives more detail than the kindergarten version shared in the birth-to-age-five section. Values about love and choice are still inserted into the description; but this also includes information about pleasure, erection, lubrication, and the movement of sperm and egg. Again, the reaction will probably be about the same for most kids in this age group: "Yuck!"

Child: **Does sex hurt?**

Q&A

Parent: Remember the clarifying questions—"What do you mean by sex?" If the child is responding to a discussion of how babies are made, you might say: "Are you asking if it hurts when a man puts his penis in a woman's vagina? When a man and a woman are kissing and touching, their bodies get excited. A man's penis will become harder; that's called an erection. A woman's vagina will get moist or a little wet. The vagina also gets bigger and smaller; it stretches. This makes it easier for the penis to fit inside the vagina without it hurting. Remember that a baby can come out of the vagina when a woman is pregnant. The way God created our bodies is pretty amazing."

During the elementary years, kids should also receive information about how and why people plan to have babies. Parents might begin by discussing intercourse apart from reproduction. It is important to fill in the gaps in children's thinking related to reproduction. Otherwise they often jump to their own conclusions. For example, many children believe their parents only have had sex as many times as the number of brothers and sisters they have. "Mom and Dad had sex twice—once for me and once for my sister." Concepts like planning pregnancies, using contraception, and having sexual intercourse for pleasure are complex. Remember, there are years to keep talking over the information. Laying the foundation and then building on information is the best educational strategy as is a good picture book (see the additional resources section at the end of this book for more information). Some phrases a parent might say to talk about intercourse and planned reproduction include:

+ "Some grown-ups choose to have intercourse even when they don't want to have a baby. It feels good and is a special way to show someone that you love them."

+ "Men and women can still have intercourse without making a baby if they prevent the sperm from reaching the egg by using things like contraception."

+ "Some men and women try to have a baby using intercourse, but the sperm and egg have trouble meeting or turning into a cell that makes a baby. Doctors can help them sometimes."

+ "Grown-ups who want to have a baby often think about things like how much time they have, how healthy they are, how much money it costs, and who in their family and community can help them take care of a baby.

+ "In some families, a woman gives birth to a baby. Other families choose to help take care of another baby that needs a family. That is called adoption."

No matter what kinds of reproduction or intercourse are discussed, a parent can share values related to choice, pleasure, and relationship commitment. The above messages also lay the foundation for discussions about safer sex practices, pregnancy prevention, and diverse families as children get older.

Relational Development

As kids grow up, their world slowly expands and how they fit in families, communities, and even the world shifts with new knowledge. Babies may only know that they are connected to parents and siblings. Then, they expand their relationships to include caregivers, extended family, and close friends. As toddlers, they make friends with a few children and begin relationships with community members in a church, teachers, and maybe even service staff at frequented stores or restaurants. Once they begin school, children start forming complex relationships with other kids and grown-ups. They are beginning to understand that they are part of a larger community. Schools teach about classrooms within the school, cities and towns within states, and countries throughout the world. At church, there are opportunities to join choir, youth group, or service projects. Kids involved in sports may start to play teams from other cities and schools. All these experiences begin to shift a child's sense of family and parent relationship as the "center of the universe."

Q&A

What should I do differently if my child has a physical or mental disability?

You know your child best. There is a spectrum of physical and mental disabilities, so there is no general answer. Some helpful points to remember are:

+ All people are sexual beings regardless of what media, doctors, or we might think.
+ Appropriate touch, love, and relationships are an important part of all our lives.
+ Children with disabilities experience sexual abuse at a higher rate than nondisabled children. Parents, caretakers, teachers, and counselors need to be aware of signs of abuse.*
+ You may need to modify or wait to provide certain developmental information to your child.
+ There are resources available. Many are specific about different types of disabilities. See the additional resources section for more information.

*Patricia Sullivan and John Knutson, "Maltreatment and Disabilities: A Population-Based Epidemiological Study," *Child Abuse & Neglect* 24, no.10 (2000): 1257–73.

The parent-child relationship is still critically important. However, it is no longer the only one and may in fact have its place of authority challenged. Ever hear, "Jayden at school says people don't go to heaven when they die, but you told me that's what happened to Grandpa." Even if Jayden's fact is something more mundane than the existence of heaven, it carries weight because your child believes Jayden. Thankfully she also trusts you to prove or disprove this new information. As a parent, you may respond, "In our faith tradition, we believe people go to heaven when they die. Not everyone shares this belief. I can't prove if Grandpa is in heaven or not, but I believe he is because Jesus taught us that we go to heaven." This answer affirms other's beliefs and your family's faith values, while also providing information. Parents' role in the elementary years is to be a role model in all their various relationships. Parents can also help kids reflect on newly forming relationships and help navigate those that may be more difficult.

> **Q&A**
>
> *Child:* **Why can't we just have a normal family?**
>
> *Parent:* What do you mean by normal family? (Wait for the answer. Normal might mean a family with a dog, a mom and dad, three kids—normal is anything your family isn't in most kid's perception.) All families are different. I know it can be difficult to want a different kind of family. But what makes family special for me is that they love and care for each other, not the number of kids or the kind of house.

In the elementary years, most children prefer to play with their own gender and can sometimes ascribe to very distinct male and female separation (boys have germs, girls have cooties). It is a very common developmental stage, but there is no definitive reason why that is so. It comes at the same point that bathrooms are divided, many sports teams become single-sex/gender, and perhaps when kids themselves, apart from culture, have a keen awareness of their bodily differences. With predominantly girls-only or boys-only friend groups, it is not uncommon to tease someone who acts in a way that does not adhere to predefined gender roles. Many elementary school children not only can identify gender roles but can articulate that gender roles are stereotypes. In other words, they push themselves and each other into these roles, but know that they are constructed. Granted, gender roles are far less constricting than they used to be, especially for girls. All children should grow up to be able to interact in positive and equal ways with both sexes/genders. Elementary school kids can have friends from just one gender group without losing opportunities to communicate and build relationships with the other gender. For example, parents can create opportunities for children to learn from grown-ups of the opposite gender, encourage friendships with both genders when possible, and model relationships across gender lines.

The gender gap may also be increasing at this age level because children are gaining a stronger sense of their self in terms of gender and body image. Trying to make sense of what it means to be a boy or girl in the world can be easy for some kids and more difficult for others. How the world perceives us as a boy or girl has a significant impact on whether a person feels that their interests, personality, and body fit with what is expected of them as a male or female. Many of these stereotypes are changing in certain parts of U.S. culture. However, many remain the same. Children who are given the chance to explore their interests in clothes, sports, music, TV shows, books, and so on, regardless of gender, often have a better sense of who they are as a person aside from gender markers. At the same time, encouraging recognition of discrimination or gender inequality is necessary so that children are not unduly harmed. For example, girls who are moved from t-ball to softball rather than baseball often wonder why they are suddenly playing a different game than boys. A family or town program may need to be sensitive to developing pride in softball equal to that of the baseball program, providing male and female coaches in both sports, and so on.

Due to the strong relationships developed with one's own gender in elementary school, children may engage in same-gender sexual exploration.[1] This is often termed "sex play" by sexuality educators. As long as the children are of the same age, it is consensual, and the play is aimed at learning what parts each person has (similar to playing doctor), this is age-appropriate and not harmful or abusive. However, if the children are more than two years apart in age, a child feels that he or she was forced to play, or a child becomes angry or shows excessive anxiety, then the behavior should be stopped immediately. Parents can help educate children about sexual abuse but can also make rules about keeping clothes on while at a friend's house or when friends are over at your house (except for dress-up time or changing to swim, for example). Even then, parents could choose to encourage privacy. In most cases, when a parent "catches" a child and playmate in sex play, the children are being doctors or scientists and learning about bodies in an imaginative and inquisitive way. Setting rules for privacy and safety are important, as is treating the incident in a calm manner that does not create shame for the children about their bodies or their actions.

The elementary school years open a whole new world of media to kids. In fact, there are whole marketing divisions specifically geared toward this age group. Media literacy—or being critical about what we see, hear, search, and learn from media—can never be taught too early. Here are some helpful hints.

+ Watch TV with your child and ask questions about the characters and story line.
+ Talk about advertising and how things often look and sound better on TV.
+ Have family discussions about a news story and bring in other perspectives.
+ Discuss how e-mail spam and Web site pop-ups work. Note that many of them contain inappropriate sexuality information for kids (and adults, to be honest!).
+ Teach children how to click off a Web site or come get you if something they did not choose pops up.
+ Bookmark specific, kid-friendly sites and allow open browsing only with an adult present.
+ Ask them what they think words or phrases mean in a popular song.

How parents react to incidents such as sex play or displays of sexuality on TV communicates how comfortable they are in dealing with sexuality issues. Elementary-age children already recognize the hushed nature of sexuality discussions or even the social taboos related to talking about sexuality. Reacting to questions in a comfortable and confident manner, as well as finding teachable moments in the six- to ten-year-old age group, helps your child see that you are open to talking about sexuality.

> **Q&A**
>
> *Child:* **Do I have to have babies when I get married?**
>
> *Parent:* Everyone makes their own choice about getting married and having babies. Some people who are married do not have children, and other people have children who are not married. It's important that you make that decision with your partner. It's a decision that you can make when you become a grown-up.

The elementary years are a great time to talk about forming relationships based on shared values. For example, parents can periodically ask children why they are friends with a particular person. Help them name common interests such as drawing, reading, or music, and also shared values such as being kind, listening to me, or letting me choose our activities sometimes. These are opportunities to describe what qualities are needed for a healthy relationship. If a child is picking friends (or being picked as a friend) based on popularity, the type of toys she has, or his new clothes, it's time to address the faith values the family has and how they affect relationship choices.

In my family, we are very clear to point out what we like about our friends and why they are our friends. We often cite examples of how they have helped others in their lives, how they treat us as friends, and how they share support of larger issues like working against racism or for peace. We do not expect our children to choose friends based on their world peace stance, but more than once I have said after a playdate, "Your friend didn't seem nice to you when you suggested a different game. How did it feel to have to play everything he wanted?" Sharing and compromise are key aspects to healthy relationships, and perhaps precursors to bringing about world peace!

The message that healthy relationships are based on positive, shared values is a key to creating gender equality and affirming gay and lesbian relationships. Kids learn that grown-up romantic relationships are healthy because of how the partners treat each other, not because they are heterosexual or homosexual. Sexual orientation and attraction information can be very basic at this age and placed within the context for relationship development. The news is ripe with stories on sexual orientation and marriage equality. There are teachable moments related to this issue in current TV shows as well. When I was a kid, I heard only about "homosexual men" once in elementary school, and I was told it was just plain wrong, no questions asked. Thankfully it was only once that I received this message that was based on hurtful and erroneous biblical interpretation. The rest of the time I was taught that how we treat each other is what's most important in God's eyes. I took that message to heart, and it is the core of my faith belief as well as the core message of the Christian love commandment. To introduce the concept of sexual orientation to elementary kids you might say:

> Many men and women are attracted to the opposite gender. Attracted means that they find them beautiful and would like to be romantic with them or be their boyfriend/ girlfriend. That is called being heterosexual. Some men are attracted to other men; that is called being homosexual or gay. Some women are attracted to women and that is called being homosexual or lesbian. Whether someone is attracted to a man or a woman is not as important as how they treat the person they love. God wants us to love and take special care of the people we are in relationships with.

For many elementary school children, same-gender relationships, such as best friends, are the first training grounds for intimate and loving relationships. This is not the same or even determinative of one's sexual orientation. It simply means that the way we love and form healthy relationships should be the same regardless of gender. Learning that lesson early will help our kids build many healthy and happy relationships in the future.

Faith Development

Elementary-age children are growing in identification with faith tradition, community, and faith practices. By the middle of elementary school, most children can identify their Christian faith tradition and its distinctiveness from other major religions as well as significant denominational differences related to practices. Membership in a faith community is often articulated by the types of activities a child engages in, such as worship on Sundays as opposed to Fridays or Saturdays, Jesus as a central figure in their faith story, Communion at different times from others, worship styles, and particular messages. Often, elementary school children see these differences similar to family origin, affiliation with a sports team, or the neighborhood one lives in. Congregational and denominational affiliation for elementary children is an identifier based on concrete differences, not deep theological divides or competing truths.

The sense of membership in a faith community provides opportunity to observe other adults' commitments to Christian values and practices.[2] It begins the process of a child connecting values

Child: How come kids never get to do anything in church besides choir? It's boring.

Parent: Many of the people at church have had to practice and learn how to help do things like read, usher, greet, and help with Communion. Is there part of church you would like to help with? (Wait for the answer, and then help your child ask someone at church how they might start learning and participating in that role.)

and actions as well as affiliation and responsibility. For example, describing what it means to be a Christian in their church, children may list the ways that their church helps the community with food or clothes drives in which they take part. There is a sense that to be a member means one participates in these important activities. Similarly, they often cite attendance at worship.

Additionally, elementary-age children begin to experience faith stories in a new way. They may still believe that the stories are literal in the sense that they could have really happened. But they are also able to infer why a faith community might tell a particular story. That is because elementary-age children can now make connections between Scripture stories and understand how stories create faith practices. For example, preschoolers can understand that Christian churches share Communion because Jesus did the same thing with his followers and we want to be like Jesus. In comparison, by the time kids are ten, they can understand the Scripture story as it connects to their church's practice of Communion, that Jesus was celebrating a Jewish tradition, and that Christian followers changed that tradition to remind us about Jesus and how much he loved us. In other words, elementary-age children are connecting the dots between Scripture, historical changes (the faith family history), and their current congregation. The Scripture stories, thus, take on a symbolic quality or serve as a template for current practices.

As children begin to identify symbols or stories used over and over in a faith tradition, they also have an increased awareness of ritual moments or ritual practice. They know Communion is more than a "nice snack" in the middle of worship. The practice connects to the tradition's stories and to the community participating together in this moment. The act of Communion then is more than what it appears to be if you were only observing the play-by-play of activity. Elementary school children begin to feel ritual in addition to knowing the actions. Exposure to rituals builds children's ability to make connections between symbol and practice and helps them grow in their relationships to God.

Prayer is another ritual opportunity if families take time to really talk about why they choose certain prayers and how they choose when to pray. Likewise, faith communities should be encouraged to develop rituals for this age group. In the Roman Catholic tradition, many children make a First Communion and Reconciliation in this age group. Protestant churches have done less to mark faith transitions for elementary children, but many host a Bible Sunday where second or third graders receive new Bibles. Rituals are moments in faith journeys when parents and religious educators help children name that faith isn't just "seen" things but also "unseen" things.

Elementary-age children are often very active and interested in the community and global service in their faith communities. This is not a surprise as it is often one of the most important ways that all children are given the opportunity to participate in the wider congregation. As children have a growing sense of membership, they seek out ways to be "members." Since many congregations let them participate in worship only in limited, preplanned ways, kids often find service projects a meaningful activity. Service projects are great teachable moments to think about ways that the love commandment is put into action in our world. Serving others as neighbor doesn't have to be "other people" in some "other place" who need help. Service projects should include helping the church congregation, doing something for members, joining with another congregation on a service project, and so on. In this way, neighbor love and service are part of forming relationships with our immediate community as well as the global community.

Connecting Our Faith and Sexuality Education

Elementary-age children notice who is popular or best at something. They have a sense that there are standards that society uses to judge people and perhaps whether they measure up or not. Church can be a place where children see themselves as loved and valued without being the best at everything. Faith communities also honor nontraditional forms of popularity like playing instruments, being studious, remembering stories, or helping others no matter who they are. We know that Jesus didn't really pick the cream of the crop to be his disciples. He probably picked people who were the last to be chosen to play kickball, or couldn't dance, or always raised their hands; the disciples were not rich, well-spoken, or smooth guys. Beyond the disciples, Jesus had a knack for ending up with the strange kid or helping the person no one wanted to talk to, let alone touch. Churches that nurture a sense of belonging for all kids, no matter who they are, model Jesus' ministry. It is countercultural, but it may just be the permission kids need to be who they really are. It honors them as uniquely created by God and valued for that.

In elementary school, kids begin to learn the history behind some Bible stories and make connections between them. For example sharing the stories of Jewish Passover, the Last Supper, and learning about a Church's Communion practice starts to lay the foundation for teaching about how Christian churches develop theology and practices based on doctrines and beliefs. Continuing to lift up stories of men and women in the Bible as models who followed God's call and made difficult choices in life gives elementary-age kids examples of what living a faithful life might mean for them. Of course a diversity of women and men is important to stress that girls and boys can equally lead and participate in God's plan. This age group can also begin to distinguish how their lives are different from the culture in which biblical characters lived (not to mention diversity of time and culture within Scripture). No one is expecting Brianna to sling shot a rock at the big bully in her school. In our culture, acting like David means that you might use your words to stand up for your friends or tell an adult that someone is being a bully.

Likewise, elementary-age children cannot start their own church like Paul, Peter, Mary, or Lydia, but they can share their faith through service projects or by participating in worship. This means that congregations need to include opportunities for kids to read during liturgy, be greeters and ushers, sing in the choir, or decorate the worship area. It is common for faith communities to allow kids to participate in worship on special Sundays. While this is wonderful and highlights how much the congregation values children, it sends a message that their participation is different and minimal. It is likely that young kids who are given opportunities to serve their congregation on a regular basis are more likely to attend worship and join in service projects as they grow into adults. It also helps them learn the practices of their faith community. For example, even adult congregants who sign up to usher have to be taught how and why the church uses ushers. Children can just as readily learn this job. An older adult can teach a younger child or have him or her shadow the adult, creating intergenerational connections. Meaningful participation by children strengthens self-esteem and self-identification with the congregation.

Service projects contribute to moral development in a number of positive ways. Congregations and parents who bring their children need to clearly articulate the values behind their service work and help kids understand why they are doing this work, giving this money, or helping these people. These acts could be connected to Christian messages such as love of neighbor, following Jesus' example in the Sermon on the Mount (Matt. 5:1–12), helping someone who is less fortunate than us like the good Samaritan (Luke 10:29–37), and so on.

Service does not need to be a scheduled event on the church calendar or family schedule. For example, a family is out at a restaurant and notices that an elderly woman and her husband are having trouble getting out the door because she has a wheelchair and he has a walker. The parent might turn to their eight-year-old daughter and ask if she thinks the couple needs help. If she agrees, the parent could suggest that she hold the door. Holding a door is something most elementary-age kids can do for other people. When she sits back down, a parent might note that her action was an example of following Jesus' directions to help our neighbors. Little by little kids learn to associate values with behaviors and make decisions about what is right or wrong in the context of the family's values. That is moral decision making. Add hundreds of tiny examples of service in a child's life together with big service projects like clothes drives and soup kitchen meals and in most cases that child will be well-equipped to make all kinds of decisions based on her values— including when to have sexual intercourse, how to treat a romantic partner, and when to become a parent.

TEACHABLE MESSAGES AND MOMENTS

God uniquely created you.

+ Puberty is how your body changes from being a kid to being a grown-up. Information is given clearly and early. Parents are a trusted comfortable source of sexuality education.
+ Gender differences exist. There is not one right way to be. Not every boy or girl, man and woman act the same way.
+ Intercourse between a man and a woman is a sexual behavior that can lead to reproduction.
+ Privacy is important as we grow older and is determined by each person.
+ Your body belongs to you, and no one is allowed to touch it without your permission.

Faith values help guide the decisions we make.

+ Opportunities for independence come with responsibility and need to be gradual.
+ Clothes reflect the way a person feels about and cares for her or his body.
+ TV shows, songs, and the Internet provide entertainment and information. They are not always correct or do not always reflect Christian values.
+ Acts of kindness and service projects put into action faith values of love of neighbor and helping the least among us.

Healthy relationships are defined by shared values, mutual decision making, and respect for each person's individuality.

+ Intercourse is a pleasurable way for two grown-ups to show that they love each other.
+ Good friendships are based on values, not popularity or the best toys.
+ Friendships are the foundation for practicing intimate healthy relationships with people outside our family.
+ Membership in a faith community involves participating in sacraments, roles in worship, and service projects.
+ The church welcomes every child and values their gifts.

REFLECTIONS

Write down a few things you learned from this chapter, some examples from your own life that reflect the teachable messages, or a reminder of something you want to do or say.

Chapter 9

Middle School Years (11–13)

Ready for Changes

Parenting Quiz

Middle school children are extremely diverse. A handful of kids may be fully physically developed but relationally struggling. Another group may seem more mature than most adults you know, but they are not yet showing visible signs of puberty. Eleven- to thirteen-year-olds are experiencing major transitions in their lives, and these may include some of the "grown-up" benefits like staying home alone; babysitting; choosing different school courses; and honing in on talents like music, sports, or art. This age group has been labeled "tweens"—no longer little children, but not yet teenagers. The answers suggested at the end are those that demonstrate comfort with sexuality issues, promote gender equality, build trust through relationship, and show that bodies deserve our care. How might you respond to the following statements or scenarios with middle school children?

1. I'm never gonna have a body that anyone notices.

   __a. Genetics can suck, but we live with what we got.

   __b. God created each of us to be different. And our bodies do amazing things; they aren't just for other people to look at.

   __c. You are beautiful/handsome. It takes a while to get comfortable with who we are, everyone goes through that process—even the airbrushed models on magazines.

   __d. Don't worry. You are good at other things. Looks aren't everything.

2. Can I have a ride to the end-of-school party at David's house?

   __a. That sounds like fun. Will David's parents be home and who is invited? I need to call over there before I make a decision.

   __b. Why don't you just take a different bus and call when you need to be picked up?

   __c. You need to tell us more about these invitations before just asking to be dropped off. We are your parents and need to know where you are and who you are with. I'll call David's parents.

   __d. Absolutely not. No parties until you are in high school.

3. Did you have a boy/girlfriend when you were my age?

   __a. I did like this one boy/girl, and I think we might have been a couple for a while. Why do you ask?

   __b. Not really, I liked a couple different people, but never dated them. Are you interested in someone at school?

   __c. You know we don't allow dating in this family.

   __d. I had lots of boy/girlfriends (or, I dated one person for two years). Only losers and nerds didn't have boy/girlfriends when I was in middle school.

4. Everyone has a smartphone. I NEED one.

    ___a. I think those phones are cool too. But until you can pay for the extra features and show how responsibly you use this phone, we won't be changing.

    ___b. If everyone jumped off a bridge, would you?

    ___c. I guess, I have one too and really love it. Let's go look this weekend.

    ___d. Smartphones are expensive. Right now you need a phone to call or text to check-in. This version will work fine.

5. Youth group is so lame. Why do I have to go?

    ___a. If you don't like something, you don't have to do it.

    ___b. I know it isn't your usual group of friends. Participating in church activities is important in our house, and youth group teaches about our faith in a different way than Sunday school.

    ___c. If you don't like what happens in youth group, why don't you meet with Pastor Jacob to talk about your ideas and hear what he has to say?

    ___d. Not everything in life is fun. So long as you live in this house, you will go to youth group.

6. Can I set up a Facebook profile?

    ___a. Facebook does not allow people under thirteen years old to create a profile. I think that is a good rule.

    ___b. Sure, I can register you, but you need to be careful.

    ___c. When you turn thirteen you can set up a profile. But we will need to sit down and talk about our family rules and general safety on Facebook before you start.

    ___d. No. Facebook is just another way for you to waste time and see things you shouldn't.

7. I guess she's my girlfriend, but I get annoyed when she calls too much.

    ___a. Just don't pick up. You don't have to respond to every call or message.

    ___b. Have you tried to talk to her about how often she calls? Do you want my help thinking about what to say?

    ___c. Girls like to talk on the phone. You'll get used to it.

    ___d. What do you think makes someone your girlfriend? (Wait for answer.) I think if someone is a girl/boyfriend, they should be able to share their feelings and talk through the problem.

Answers: 1: b, c; 2: a, c; 3: a, b; 4: a, d; 5: b, c; 6: a, c; 7: b, d

Growing and Changing

Tweens are in early adolescence. Puberty has begun at a time when they become much more self-centered in their focus. They may experience feelings of attraction and experiment with sexual behaviors like kissing and touching. Yet parents are still an important part of their lives and decision making. Friends are given increasing importance as tweens work through where they will fit in the scope of community life. Parents might think about adolescence as prolonged toddlerhood—only this time it is about dating, schoolwork, phones, cars, and job responsibilities. Setting clear boundaries and giving kids a sense of independence within the family structure helps them form healthy relationships and take responsibility for their behaviors through middle adolescence and into the young adult years of late adolescence.

Physical Development

The changes that accompany puberty can make any child feel nervous or anxious, especially given the diversity of experiences of their peers. Middle school kids may have a low buzz in the back of their brain asking when it will happen, how it will occur, how they can be prepared, and so on. Most middle school-age kids live with myths and hopes about puberty—some stories have an urban-legend quality like getting your period while wearing white pants and others hold a time-honored truth like dealing with a spontaneous erection in class or secretly wearing a bra, but hoping no one notices. Kids try to measure themselves against a "normal puberty" that does not exist.

Puberty is the transition the body makes to being able to reproduce or make a baby. There are averages that reflect when most U.S. children will start developing secondary sex characteristics, such as hair under arms and around external genitals, deepening of the voice and growth of the penis and testicles for males, breast buds begin and nipples grow darker for females, increased sweating, growth spurt in height, filling out of girls' hips, and so on. Average does not equate to normal, and a number of factors, like weight, diet, genetics, and even environment, contribute to differences in when and how physical changes will occur. Due to these changes, kids and parents become aware of increased hygiene needs. Wearing deodorant and showering more often are two ways that a youth can take responsibility in response to physical changes. Tweens may also begin to experience mood swings because of changing hormone levels. General moody, feisty, or sassy behavior cannot be blamed on hormones. More rapid swings, including strong shows of emotion, may be partly in response to hormone changes. There is no excuse for rude or disrespectful behavior at any time. However, a bit of understanding and patience may help a tween understand how to better respond to shifts in mood.

Q&A

Girl: **Can I stay home from school? I have my period.**

Parent: I know that having your period can make you feel sore or even a little sick, but it is a normal part of life and the way our bodies were created. If you feel awkward because of your period, that is probably because you know about it. Very few other people will even notice. You can always take some pain relievers to see if that helps. (In some cases, young women experience severe cramps and nausea from menstruating. If so, take your daughter to her pediatrician or an ob-gyn to have this treated.)

The average age for menarche (first period) is about twelve-and-one-half years old in the United States; spermarche (development of sperm in the testes) is experienced anywhere from eleven to fifteen, with an average of thirteen-and-one-half years old, though little research has been conducted on this.

In middle school, kids should have a complete understanding of menstruation, erections, and ejaculation. In the elementary years, biological facts are shared about these processes more so than the experience and preparation for them. A pamphlet, book, or even a trusted online resource may be helpful to parents as they set aside time to discuss this special and amazing change in our bodies. Both boys and girls need this information. Teaching both boys and girls about menstruation, erections, and ejaculation reduces the joke telling, misinformation, and lack of gender awareness that some middle school children experience.

Menstruation may occur in young women before they have actually ovulated. It is the body's process of getting the uterus ready for a fertilized egg each month if needed. Hormones called progesterone and estrogen ebb and flow in a communication system with the body, telling it to build up the tissue, mostly water and a little blood in the uterus. If an egg is not implanted, the uterus contracts (called cramps) to release and push the extra tissue out of the uterus. Middle school kids need to know that the tissue is often different colored and flows lighter and heavier at times. It is not like a cut where blood gushes out. Being prepared for the type of fluid can reduce panic and prevent concerns.

In this refresher conversation on menstruation, a parent can now add information on how to prepare for a period. Having items to touch and look at helps teach kids that though these products need to be clean, they are not shameful or secretive. Pads or sanitary napkins as well as tampons now come in "teen-friendly" packages. However, small sizes of traditional pads and tampons work just as well. For a daughter, a parent might purchase a special container for tampons or a small coin purse to hold pads. Make sure that she knows where to find these materials in the house and public restrooms when needed. Having these in a backpack or locker often reduces the fear that periods come with no warning and are very heavy. In fact, many periods begin with light spotting and bodily changes like excess water, upset stomach, or headache which help to notify a girl that she will likely begin her period soon. Keeping a menstruation journal for the first year of a girl's period can help a young woman recognize these signals and feelings as well as determine if she has a regular cycle. Empowering kids to know their bodies well and take care of them as part of God's gift includes their sexual and reproductive health.

Erections can be an even more awkward social experience for boys than the experience that girls have when they think that everyone is watching them grab their purse with a pad or tampon in it before walking to the bathroom. Most often males experience an erection because they are aroused by a thought, person, image, or experience. The muscles at the base of the penis contract and blood flow increases to the penis, causing it to swell and become erect. Males are capable of erections from the time that they are born; even some ultrasounds have claimed to show male fetuses with an erection. An erection in the morning is often caused by a full bladder causing the muscles to contract. Erections increase during puberty as boys begin to experience feelings of attraction and sexual desire. Yet erections can also happen for no reason at all. It is extremely important that both boys and girls are taught this fact. Many grown men tell stories about a time when they got an erection in class, church, or camp that resulted in humiliation, ridicule, and shame. Erections are a bodily response, not one that is easily controlled, especially for middle school boys.

Q&A

Child: **Dad, what's erectile dysfunction?**

Parent: You already know that penises can become hard or erect. For some men this stops happening and they may take medicine if they still want to have sexual intercourse or make a baby. I don't think that we need to see commercials about it during every sports game, but the advertisers know that lots of men watch sports and they want to sell the medicine to them.

Ejaculation is a separate, but related, topic to erection. Girls and boys need to know what spermarche is and when it may happen. Explain that this means a male's testicles are starting to make sperm due to changes in the hormone levels (mostly testosterone) in his body. The sperm travel from the testicles through a number of tubes and glands where it is mixed with fluid to help nourish it. Having a book or looking at a diagram online helps with all the names like vas deferens, epididymis, and seminal vesicles. Semen is made up of sperm and seminal fluid to help keep the sperm alive. The semen comes out the urethra of the penis the same way that urine comes out. The body closes off the opening between the bladder and the urethra so that urine cannot get into the semen.

After this review of sperm production, boys also need to be prepared for the time when an erection leads to ejaculation. Parents can convey that often the first ejaculation will happen at night and many people call this a wet dream. Then discuss with your son what to do with sheets and pajamas when and if this happens. Make sure that he is comfortable with the plan and knows that ejaculation is a natural bodily function.

The major changes in the body can lead any middle school child to feel awkward. Parents who take the time to prepare their child for these changes by providing factual, reassuring, and realistic information may transform the shame and discomfort experienced at puberty into awe and anticipation. Middle school kids are also at a point where they are beginning to think that they "should know everything already." They may be less likely to ask about the finer details of menstruation, picking a bra, having a nocturnal emission, or wearing deodorant than a parent had hoped. Even the most open and loving parent may need to take the lead in sharing sexuality information and providing safe places for kids to find their own information when needed. Health-care professionals are partners in sharing sexual health information at this age as well. Kids should have time alone with their doctor or nurse at this age to discuss sexuality issues or any questions they may have regarding physical or emotional issues.

Middle school-age kids often begin to experience their first feelings of sexual attraction. This may be a crush on a person in school, an adult teacher, a movie star or music artist, or all the above. A parent might share a story about a first crush or someone who they found attractive in school to open the conversation to discussing sexual desire and attraction. Desire and attraction are feelings of wanting to be with or close to someone. We feel desire and attraction toward a number of things, including food and entertainment. Our body reacts to things it finds pleasing. Just like we can decide not to eat ten chocolate bars or to turn off the third episode in a row of our favorite television show, we can appreciate our feelings for someone without acting on them. For example, a parent in a monogamous relationship might share that they still find other people attractive (name a movie star, sports figure, or stranger walking down the street), but because of their commitment to their partner they don't act on those attractions.

Feelings of sexual attraction often mean that middle school kids will begin dating and with that may come initial sexual behaviors like kissing and touching. It is a small percentage of kids thirteen and under who engage in sexual intercourse and oral sex. On average in the United States, about 6 percent of youth under thirteen have had vaginal intercourse, which further breaks down to 3 percent for girls and 8 percent for boys.[1] This is often with an older partner.

Regardless of whether or not middle school kids are engaging in sexual behaviors, they are able to understand the need for contraception and safer sex practices. In early adolescence, children tend to have a more concrete worldview about what is right and wrong. Teaching about safer sex practices as the right way to keep yourself and a partner safe is a clear message that middle school kids comprehend. Similar to conversations about menstruation, showing a few examples of contraception and barrier methods—like what is done with tampons and pads—help kids understand just how these methods work.

Showing a child how a condom works does not increase their likelihood to engage in sexual intercourse. That is a myth. What it may do is give him or her the confidence to use a condom when she or he does decide to engage in sexual intercourse. Local Planned Parenthood centers and online sites have pamphlets that discuss a variety of contraceptive and sexually transmitted disease prevention methods. Bring a pamphlet home and share it with your youth. Church leaders can have this information in their office and in public places in the church mixed in with other pamphlets dealing with loss, cancer, welcoming new members, and so forth.

Q&A

I don't want my child to have premarital sex. How can I make sure that they don't?

You can't. That is your child's decision to make. You can do your best to give them information to make an informed decision, support them so they will come to you when trying to make that decision, and create safe dating practices so they don't feel pressured into the decision.

Discussing safer sex practices provides an opportunity to discuss positive limit setting for sexual behaviors. In middle school, masturbation may be intended for sexual pleasure and exploration. It is also a great alternative to early engagement in sexual behaviors with another person. Many parents may want to make a hard and fast rule about what sexual behaviors will be acceptable and which ones will not (perhaps up until the time of marriage). This is both unrealistic and misses a significant chance to help with your child's sexual development. Healthy and responsible adults know that teens will have sexual feelings, but they don't have to act on them. They also know that engaging in a variety of sexual behaviors in a relationship—starting with less intimate behaviors—is a way to build trust, excitement, and knowledge about each other. Youth can start doing this in their very first relationships. For example, a couple needs to figure out for themselves when it feels right to hold hands, ask the other person's permission, and sometimes choose not to hold hands (even if they already have at other times). This is positive limit setting.

Kids generally know how to assess timing and privacy of sexual behaviors, although this doesn't make them any less nervous. Years of watching TV and other adults help them to figure out the basics. Youth often consider how long a couple has been together, age of partners, setting for the date, and each person's values before deciding what sexual behaviors are appropriate. For example, most kids will say a thirteen- and fourteen-year-old who have been going out for two weeks might kiss, but that's all they should do. Whereas a sixteen- and seventeen-year-old who have been going out for a month, might kiss, touch each other's bodies, and even take some clothes off. This isn't scientific data, just what I tend to hear at youth group workshops I lead.

Kids also need to know that each relationship is different and that a parent is willing to talk through these decisions. Parents have to engage youth in conversations that elicit this information or help them think through it more explicitly. For example, a parent might see someone kissing on TV and ask, "Those people just met. How long do you think you need to know someone before you kiss that person romantically?" Sprinkle in these kinds of questions and observations throughout middle school, and by high school, kids have a pretty good sense of when to say yes to some behaviors and no to others.

Q&A

Child: **Can I please to go the movie on Friday with Kai? Angela and Julian are going too.**

Parent: I appreciate your coming to ask and tell me about Kai. I/We need to talk to Kai's parents first. And you need to tell me which movie, what time, and who is dropping off and picking up. If you can plan the evening responsibly, we support your going. You haven't known Kai for more than a few weeks. I'm curious about how you think the date will go? What do you hope will happen?

Relational Development

By middle school, most kids have gained a measure of independence. They can get on and off the bus or walk to and from events by themselves. They take care of their daily tasks and chores with fewer reminders and assistance from adults. They also become interested in more grown-up aspects of life like the news, popular music, fashion, sports, and books. Parents may suddenly find that their middle school youth is joining adult conversations. In response, parents might "let go" or "become friends" with their youth. There is a sense of relief and a break from the more than a decade of parental duties. Other parents might have the exact opposite reaction. In many ways middle school kids are still children, and some parents do not want them to grow up and lose their little boy or girl.

Like every stage of development, middle school is as much a relationship transition for parents as it is for kids. However, the basics of the parent-child relationship do not need to change. Parents are still parents. Kids are still kids. Middle school youth still need a routine and parental limit setting that includes expectations for faith practices, friendships, dating, and contributions to the family. Middle school youth will begin to push against rules and limits. That is their developmental role, and frankly it is how they test their own decisions.

Puberty can cause stress as kids realize that their identity is changing. Physically they are changing. What will they look like? They also are changing roles from a child to an adult. Don't be surprised if one minute a middle school child is playing a child's game and the next minute watching the evening news. Similar to toddlerhood, this is a *both-and* stage of life, which can be liberating and frustrating. The physical, psychological, and cognitive development that happens in adolescence is only rivaled by early infancy and toddler years. Dealing with this confusion explains much of why tweens and teens appear to be preoccupied with, well frankly, themselves!

Middle school-age kids have more adult sensibilities like

understanding jokes with sexual content, the harm of gender stereotypes, and ways that race and class affect people's ability to live equal lives. These recognitions bring about feelings of self-consciousness. For example, cooties are no longer the motivation to maintain gender lines. Now the pressure may be based on a cultural belief that girls who act too much like boys (sporty, smart, outspoken, and free-spirited) will be seen as unattractive or aggressive. Boys who act too much like girls (thoughtful, caring, well-groomed, and attentive to rules) will be seen as sissies or momma's boys.

$Q_{&}A$

Child: **A kid at school said someone was gay. What does that mean?**

Parent: Being gay means that a boy or man is attracted to another boy or man. Some women are attracted to other women, too. They are called lesbian. There are also people who are attracted to men and women; that is called bisexual. Attracted is when someone likes the way another person looks or acts and wants them to be their boyfriend or girlfriend. Do you think that the kid said the other boy was "gay" to be mean? (Wait for the answer.) Some people think it is wrong to like someone of the same gender or sex. But who we are attracted to is part of how God created us, and as long as we treat each other with respect and love, it does not matter if the two people are two boys, two girls, or a girl and boy. If the kid used the word *gay* to mean stupid or unpopular, it is disrespectful and rude because it's like using a specific person as a stand-in for the word *stupid.*

With regard to sexuality, harmful gender stereotypes weave through and tangle the process of a child forming a healthy sexual self-concept. A sexual self-concept is an individual's understanding of their sexuality as God created her or him to be in the world. This involves knowing what our sense of gender and sexual orientation are. What kind of girl or boy am I? What kind of people am I attracted to (in regard to both which sex and what personalities)? How does all this fit with what my culture says about sexuality? Sexual self-concept changes as we form new relationships, our bodies change, or we experience different events and behaviors. It is a process.

Middle school kids wonder if their sexuality is normal if they masturbate, have wet dreams, haven't had their period yet, have a girlfriend, or lack interest in dating. Tweens may experiment with games like spin the bottle or seven minutes in heaven with friends as a way to learn how to kiss, for example. In most cases these games are about experimentation, not exploitation. Mature sexual behaviors involving intercourse and oral sex introduce emotional and physical risks that are beyond the scope of any game. Tweens need to know that they can say no to any sexual behavior or social situation that makes them uncomfortable or feels coercive, and that you would pick them up anywhere at any time. Each person's sexuality is unique to them and is a good part of God's creation. Repeating that often and with deep sensitivity will help support a positive body image, as well as provide confidence in their gender identity, sexual orientation, and myriad relationships.

A significant amount of work has been done in the United States to boost young girls' self-esteem and life options. A growing movement of "girls can do anything" is as much market driven as gospel truth. However, boys have not had the same attention paid to them. One reason might be because the "grrrl" model is built on a very masculine stereotype that boys are already emulating. Another reason may be that more social benefits befall boys, and they get by for the most part only partially scathed by locker room harassment, high school cliques, and general humiliation.

In reality, bullying and negative messages related to body image, gender, and sexual orientation harm girls and boys. *All* children need to hear that they are loved and supported no matter their body type, gender identity, or sexual orientation. Creating spaces that affirm a variety of gender expressions help tweens believe the message that they are loved by God and created to be unique, amazing individuals. The United Church of Christ has created a Web site to help Christian churches address bullying in youth groups and school, which can be found in the additional resources list at the end of the book.

Bullying is often a product of the peculiar group expression of egocentricity in adolescent development. Instead of turning into radical individualists, many kids join groups of friends, model a style or click together, and determine uniqueness by fitting into one group over and against the other seventeen available lunch tables. In other words, the obsession with "me" comes hand-in-hand with a desire to fit into a group. It is not until late teen years that kids are able to understand themselves in relation to others without having to be just like the other person. This psychosocial development may come through in a teen's ability to form value judgments that go against the group norm, move beyond "falling-in-love" every time they meet a new person, and maintain many relationships at the same time, including family, friends, and a romantic relationship.

The tween years are a primary time to start testing and developing intense friendships and dating as well as gaining more independence from family. They want to spend more time with friends and give greater significance to BFF (best friend forever) relationships. Relationship balance is front and center as kids begin to cut off parents or reject siblings in an attempt to give their friends greater priority. Suddenly, pizza and movie night with the family is "so uncool." Simply pointing out these behavior and value changes help tweens to see the shift in their relationships. For example, a parent might say, "It seems like hanging out with your friends has become more important to you than spending time with family. Just like we can have more than one friend at a time, we can like our friends and family at the same time too." In other words, friends can be very important, but that doesn't mean family has to be less important or less loved. It just means time needs to be shared in a different way.

Dating Violence

In dating relationships, teens can become very other-focused. Excitement and delight in another person's affection is a typical reaction as a teen (and an adult). When the dating relationship becomes controlling, violent, or damaging to their self-esteem, tweens and teens need to be able to recognize the signs, such as

+ physical violence (like pinching, hitting or slapping, kicking, choking)
+ sexual violence (like unwanted touching, pressure to engage in behaviors, forced sexual acts)
+ emotional abuse (like yelling, insults, threats, controlling friendships or choices, jealousy, checking personal texts/ e-mails/Facebook)

Teen dating abuse can be experienced by any teen, including the wealthy and underprivileged; white teens and racial/ethnic teens; and those living in the suburbs, country, or urban areas. About one in eleven teens reports being a victim of physical abuse each year, while one in four reports experiencing verbal, emotional, or sexual abuse. Perhaps more startling, one in three teens reports knowing a friend or peer who has been hit, punched, kicked, slapped, choked, or otherwise physically hurt by his or her partner. Many adults do not see this violence even though it is most likely to take place in one of the partner's homes. One reaction might be to ask why teens don't just break up with the other person. In abusive relationships, teens report partners threatening violence or self-harm when presented with a breakup.[2]

Parents should share the warning signs of abuse and talk through how your tween/teen or their friends can seek help when/if needed. No one can ever fully prevent violence or abuse if another person is intent on causing harm. Some people in churches may even use Scripture to condone violence against women or mistreatment of gay, lesbian, and transgender youth. The love commandment is clear that the way we love our girl/boyfriend needs to be with the same care as if it were God or ourselves. That love does not abuse or have power over. Tweens and Teens need to hear messages about dating like: everyone deserves respect and love does not cause harm.

Similarly intense friendships in middle school are often the modeling ground for future romantic relationships. What makes a good friend eventually makes for a good partner. When I say this to a middle school youth group, they inevitably raise the volume with "Gross, I'm not going to date my friend." Their concrete thinking and literal brains often latch onto a direct link between the friend next to them and dating. I assure them that is not what I mean, even if they might someday find themselves dating their current friends. I pass out a piece of paper that has a list of qualities and activities with one column that says friend and another that says lover. I ask them to check off friend and/or lover for each quality or activity that matches. Inevitably, by the end of the exercise most kids have two overlapping columns with things double checked like share feelings, support each other in new activities, spend time alone together, hang out with different friends, talk about faith and beliefs, share common music and TV interests, and go places together. Then there are some variations. Most tweens don't think a lover should help them with their chores but a friend would. They don't have pet names for friends, but they might for lovers. Other tweens say nicknames are fine for both, but pet names are silly in both cases. Sexual behaviors like kissing, hugging, and touching are for lovers not friends. When the exercise is over and we've reviewed the overlapping qualities and activities versus the differences, I ask if anyone noticed anything. Thankfully, someone in the group always says, with a little surprise in their voice, "So, like, a lover is a lot like a friend or at least should be." Bingo!

Most U.S. youth date at some point during their adolescence (ages eleven through early twenties). Dating relationships can be as different and diverse as the kids involved. Some may last a few days, a few weeks, even months, and occasionally over a year. Early adolescents or tweens may not begin formally dating. Many go out in groups of friends where one or two pairs are "seeing each other." Nearly three in four tweens report "boyfriend/girlfriend relationships usually begin at age 14 or younger."[3] Some sexuality experts suggest discouraging intense one-on-one romantic relationships and older partners (more than two years age difference) in early adolescence because of a lack of social and emotional development, as well as the potential for early mature sexual behaviors and abuse.[4] But going to a dance together, talking on the phone, going out to movies with groups of friends, or spending supervised time at each other's homes are typical tween behaviors and part of healthy adolescent development.

Q&A

Child: **Boys are always joking about girls and talking about their bodies.**

Parent: It doesn't matter if someone is a boy or girl. It's disrespectful to talk about body parts like they are objects separate from the person. I hope you will say something when you hear a boy making a rude comment or joke. God wants us to celebrate each other's beauty, and saying someone is beautiful or handsome is a compliment. But jokes can be hurtful.

Parents and youth leaders are important models for teens. They watch and learn from parents and other trusted adults how to negotiate and balance relationships. Talking with tweens honestly and providing them with accurate information will help them stay safe, develop healthy romantic relationships, and create a balance within all their relationships. Dating is not simple, and there is not just one way to do it. In fact, many adolescents will date multiple people throughout adolescence. When tweens are in a new, intense, and singularly focused relationship, they do not often see the hard work that it will take to maintain a relationship. Parents and youth leaders can be supportive and instructive by taking youth friendships and dating relationships seriously, while simultaneously recognizing that there will be other (perhaps better) relationships in the future.

Faith Development

Adolescents seek independence in family relationships and also in faith relationships. Middle school youth not only have a sense about their faith tradition as different from others, but also begin to develop a sense of ownership of their faith. They may start to distinguish why they choose to be this faith or that faith and yet they are equally apt to question their personal faith tradition. In order to support the process of adolescent moral development, especially related to sexual decision making, tweens need space to question.

Youth who have the opportunity to sift through family values and faith beliefs will have a better sense of their meaning and history to the family or faith community. For some parents, this may seem like letting kids pick and choose what values they like or don't like. That's not the intention. Youth need and want to know the values of their traditions. When values are not clearly stated, youth do not know exactly what they are being asked to accept. Parents and youth leaders create a delicate balance between telling youth what is right and wrong and telling them *why* the church believes it is right or wrong, *how* over history it came to these beliefs, and *why* they should wrestle with these conclusions even if they do not like them or agree with them. This is the practice of ethical thinking. As a result, tweens take major steps in their moral development as they are allowed to learn to question and accept values and beliefs in their faith tradition.

Tweens are still very concrete thinkers with a sense of right and wrong as black and white. They are most likely to believe the "rules of a church" without much questioning. However, their sense of nuance is growing. Tweens still value the story part of Scripture, but they start to see the way these stories fit within a "big picture," including learning about the history of the people and places where the Scripture was written. For example, the "story" that Jesus washed his disciples' feet (John 13:1–17) teaches us about service to others. When kids talk about the Scripture

Talking about Technology

Online communication increases and archives the common issues tweens and teens face in non-cyber life. The late night phone call, the double dare, or the paper note full of sexual innuendo have been replaced by text messages, e-mail, and Facebook posts. The *Playboy* or *Playgirl* magazine found in a dumpster or an older sibling's room is now available at the click of a mouse. Technology allows for endless possibility; it can also bring greater legal and social consequences.

Sex + Texting = Sexting

Sexting is the act of sending, receiving, or forwarding naked photos or comments via a mobile phone. It can include posting pictures and comments on social networking sites. What teens (and many adults) often don't understand is that once a photo is sent via phone, e-mail, or posted on a social networking site, it can be forwarded and reposted without consent. In many states this behavior falls under child pornography laws and can have major ramifications if a teen is legally charged with a crime.

One in ten girls ages thirteen to sixteen have "electronically sent or posted nude or semi-nude images of themselves."[5] One in three teen boys and one in four teen girls have had a nude or semi-nude photo shared with them when they were not the intended recipient. While "sexting" is more prevalent than we would like to admit, it is more likely that your teen is not sending sexually suggestive material. Having a conversation early will help your tween know not only legal issues related to sexting but also what your expectations are!

Pornography

Finding online pornography is easy. In fact, sometimes it finds you, through pop-up ads and spam e-mail messages. Research published in *Pediatrics* found that four of ten tweens and teens visited a sexually explicit site in the last year. While boys were more likely than girls to seek out pornography, two-thirds of the time exposure to images was unwanted.[6] Researcher Ralph DiClemente studies the effects of media on youth sexual perceptions and behaviors. His findings suggest that use of online pornography by youth may skew their understanding of bodies, sexual behaviors, and relationships. Other studies have suggested that teens who seek out online pornography are more likely than their counterparts to view sex as recreational and women as sexual objects.[7]

+ + +

Parents can talk to their kids about healthy and safe ways to use new technologies. Here are some parental messages and practices:

+ Teen sexting and online pornography use have potentially severe legal ramifications. Teens need to hear why sending or viewing sexually explicit material not only is a poor legal decision but also is counter to values of honesty, consent, and mutuality in relationships.

+ Everything on the Internet is potentially public. Once tweens send something, it is archived and retrievable. Additionally, more and more schools and employers are researching potential students/employees online, particularly on their social networking sites. Instill that these types of interactions can affect them even years in the future.

+ Not all sexual material is pornography. Tweens and teens can understand the difference between mutual erotic material and violent, sexist pornography. This distinction may be helpful to teens as they become young adults in healthy and loving relationships—where use of erotic materials may enhance a couples' sexual relationship.

+ Parents can institute random checks on cell phone text messages or social networking sites. Look through them with your child present: secret checks do not instill trust. When nothing unseemly pops up, kids should be complimented for their responsible use of technology. If inappropriate pictures or language is used, parents can follow through on consequences like having your child pay a portion of the bill or losing access to one's phone or computer.

+ Parents can provide a list of bookmarked Web sites that give accurate information about sexual health, sexual behaviors, and relationships. This avoids open searches that often turn up pornographic pop-ups or portals to such Web sites.

along with the historical fact that people wore sandals on dirt roads for days at a time without washing and that religious leaders usually had other people (lower than them) wash their feet, Jesus' act of service carries new meaning. It shows that he was willing to make himself an equal to or less than his disciples by society's standards. He was also willing to get dirty to show his love for them.

Unlike elementary school-age kids who start to put a few stories together and recognize themes, middle school kids can gather core values and see that the text itself brings new insights and greater meaning into their lives. It means something to them on a different level.[8] They are moving toward the faith tradition not just as "a family history" but a history of which they are choosing (or not) to be a part.

In the middle school years, relationships are tested with parents, and friends are given greater priority. A prayer relationship with God can get lost in that mix. Not to mention what questioning of faith values and traditions might do to one's belief in God generally. Unless there has been a crisis in a child's life, up to this point most kids have not questioned God's goodness or love of them. They may not have a particularly close relationship with God, either, but God is still God because other people say so. Early adolescence is a time when God can seem distant, cruel (puberty might seem like a curse), or even made up. An awareness of the larger world brings with it questions about natural disasters, creation and evolution, and why some religions hurt people intentionally. Middle school-age youth need role models for bringing these questions to God in prayer. They are ready to hear that faith isn't easy. Just like any relationship, one with God takes practice and patience.

Connecting Our Faith and Sexuality Education

Scripture is filled with stories about love and relationships. The events are not always culturally relevant to our time, nor do they always have happy endings. Middle school-age kids no longer believe these stories in their literal sense. They are able to grasp the meaning behind and within the stories for their faith lives. In the creation stories tweens can recognize that gender distinctions have more to do with the cultural context out of which the story comes than God intending unequal gender roles. In the first creation stories in Genesis, male and female are created at the same time and named good (Gen. 1:27). The second creation story in Genesis 2 shows God's concern that the first human, Adam, was alone (v. 18). God tries all kinds of animals as partners to make Adam happy (2:19-20). At last, it is another human being that Adam sees as his partner (2:23). The message for tweens is that God created humans to be social and share love.

The love commandment is the golden rule for Christian relationships: "'You shall love the Lord your God with all your heart, and with all your soul, and with all your strength, and with all your mind; and your neighbor as yourself'" (Luke 10:27). Middle school kids can evaluate relationships based on the love commandment both from Scripture and from their lives. Where do they see God in a relationship? How is a person showing that they love themselves and that they love their neighbor? Parents and youth leaders could have kids practice by highlighting the positive and negative sides of romantic love and friendships in stories like Jacob, Leah, and Rachel (Gen. 29); David and Bathsheba (2 Sam. 11-12), David and Jonathan (1 Sam. 20); Ruth and Naomi (Ruth 1-4); Mary and Joseph (Matt. 1-2; Luke 2); and Jesus and the Disciples (Luke 5:1-11; John 13:1-20; Mark 14:43-52). In these types of exercises, youth are identifying healthy and unhealthy values or practices in a relationship; they are not pretending that relationships in ancient Israel are models for current romantic partnerships.

Many middle school-age youth questioning their faith are drawn to stories like the Prodigal Son (Luke 15:11-32) and Doubting Thomas (John 20:24-29). The parable of the prodigal son lets them see that even if they make mistakes or leave God and faith for a while, they will be welcomed back. Doubting Thomas is a character that asks what every person of faith has wondered at some point—how can I believe if I have no proof? Talking about Thomas with tweens allows parents to share a personal faith crisis or acknowledge that questioning does not make a person weak or less Christian. It may actually mean a youth is working hard to be faithful and is looking for concrete ways to see Jesus in their life. For many middle school youth, this may come in the form of service projects, a faith sponsor/mentor, or having a particular prayer answered.

Repeating earlier childhood messages about God blessing creation as good supports positive body image during puberty and also acknowledges that diversity and difference are intended by God. Bodies have been a controversial and contentious topic in the Christian tradition. The two most popular strains of thought are: one, the body is a temple to be revered and set apart; two, it is an animal-like quality standing in the way of a spiritual life. Some Christians respond to these messages by either promoting control of bodies or completely denying them.

God, in the form of Jesus, came to the world as a human being, body and all! Jesus did not disdain his body. He ate with friends, touched those who needed healing, journeyed for miles with companions, and had his feet anointed. Surely he followed the custom of his day and danced with, kissed, hugged, and slept in the same space as his companions. These are all examples of Jesus' expression of his embodiment (a body and soul together) and of his sexuality. They are not sexual in the way we think of sexual behaviors toward someone to whom we are attracted. For youth, what is important is that Jesus lived an embodied life as our God, just as we are called to respect and care for our bodies.

The need to be touched in loving and appropriate ways is part of who we are. When we do not have healthy examples of touch or we have no touch at all, our body image and our ability to share intimacy are damaged. Honoring our bodies as "very good" means learning to love our own body (body image) and learning to share our body with others in loving ways. There are limits to how we ought to use our bodies. Those limits are not because there is something wrong with "flesh." Those limits reflect Christian values of respect for creation, not harming others, and responsibility for our community and relationships.

Q&A

Child: **When did you first have sex?**

Parent: The decision to have sexual intercourse with someone is a personal choice. The details of that choice are a private matter, even for me. What I hear you asking is, "how do you know when you are ready?" I think two people have to know a lot about each other so that their decision is made together and talked about a lot. They have also usually tried other sexual behaviors, and they can handle how intercourse might change their relationship, including protecting against pregnancy if this is a heterosexual relationship and also protecting against disease. I also think that sexual intercourse changes how the two people feel about each other, and that isn't something that can ever go back to the way it was. It's a big decision that I hope you wait to make until you are out of high school.

Your child may never be comfortable asking you this question, even though it is often the question that parents dread. Other ways to bring this subject up include teachable moments like reflecting on a book, film, or TV character; referencing a popular song; or just saying, "I wish someone had told me."

Similarly, the Christian tradition has struggled with what it should say about marriage. Often youth do not receive any formal education in faith communities about marriage or parenting. Starting in middle school, youth begin to think more seriously about their future lives (if still in fairy tale terms). Parents who share their values about marriage and are realistic about the work it takes to be parents prepare their children to think critically about their future. Most Christian churches are making significant theological shifts in their marriage teachings. They now understand marriage to be based on love, support inclusion of same-sex partners, and affirm sexual pleasure as part of healthy sexual relationships. Thus, marriage is defined by values present in the relationships and how strengths and weaknesses balance each other—rather than by solely the union of a man or woman.

For example, my husband and I did not determine household duties by who was male and who was female. We talked through who had which strengths, skills, and desires for different activities. We can both mow a lawn. But my spouse loves to green up a yard, pull weeds, and mulch, things about which I am not passionate. My spouse is also very organized about grocery shopping and stocking the fridge. I, on the other hand, enjoy cooking. I also like to buy presents and write thank-you notes. So I keep track of the birthday parties and the gifts received. We share the parental duties of child care equally, including homework, bedtime rituals, morning routines, and so on.

These are small examples—some correspond to our assigned cultural gender roles, but they were not chosen because of them. We are also not rigid about who has to do them. In fact, we consciously talk about these decisions in front of our children. Open communication and mutual decision making are critical elements of a healthy, long-term relationship. Modeling or talking about these qualities help youth identify them in their own relationships. Kids live in a culture where marriage is discussed on a daily basis. This discussion usually centers around who is allowed to get married or what kind of weddings celebrities have. Kids don't often get a realistic picture of the hard work and emotional investment that go into maintaining, evaluating, and sometimes ending long-term relationships. It doesn't matter if a parent is married, divorced, or has never been married. Hearing from a variety of adults about marriage starts kids on the road to intentionally thinking through their own ideas about marriage.

TEACHABLE MESSAGES AND MOMENTS

Bodies are amazing parts of creation.

+ Reinforce messages about positive body image.
+ Prepare for menstruation and nocturnal emissions.
+ Support gender equality in messages and behaviors.
+ Affirm sexual attraction and desire as part of who we are.
+ Promote safety and care, which includes being knowledgeable about safer sex practices.

Questioning is a way of growing and deepening our faith.

+ Talk about faith values in clear and concrete ways.
+ Show how faith values have changed over time, especially related to our bodies, gender, and sexual orientation.
+ Promote participating in service projects or finding an adult mentor in the faith community.

Balancing relationships is the key to the love commandment.

+ Reinforce maintaining multiple friends and family relationships (don't need to sacrifice one for the other).
+ Be clear. Parents are parents, and kids are kids. Don't confuse the roles.
+ Take friendships and dating seriously, but discourage long-term dating.
+ Create supportive opportunities for greater independence (such as the use of technology).
+ Talk through decisions about dating and relationships, using TV shows or real-life scenarios.

REFLECTIONS

Write down a few things you learned from this chapter, some examples from your own life that reflect the teachable messages, or a reminder of something you want to do or say.

Chapter 10

High School Years (14–18)

On the Journey

Parenting Quiz

Developmentally, middle adolescents or high school students are going through a process of becoming more independent and developing wider networks of relationships. Their primary relationships once based in the family with parents and siblings are replaced by friendships and romantic partners in a more or (often) less graceful way. Whether in a dating relationship or not, teens spend a significant amount of time thinking about, planning for, and working through romantic relationships. They seem to already "know everything." If your teen is acting this way, don't worry, they're supposed to! The answers suggested at the end are those that demonstrate comfort with sexuality issues, promote gender equality, build trust through relationships, and show that bodies deserve our care. How might you respond if your quirky, unruly, brooding, and sometimes thoughtful teen said or asked the following?

1. I have a zit; I can't go to school!
   a. I know it makes you uncomfortable, but school is important for your future, and you cannot miss it because of a zit.
   b. OMG, should I call the doctor?
   c. There are people dying of hunger, unable to attend school all over the world, and you're worried about a zit.
   d. You have great friends. They will still like you if you have a zit, and anyone who doesn't isn't a true friend.

2. What do you like about your job?
   a. I hate working, and I'd do it less if I didn't have to pay for a house and kids.
   b. Work is called that because it isn't fun for me. I get enjoyment from my hobbies and volunteering.
   c. I'm blessed to have a job where I do things that interest me. I like (name one specific example).
   d. Study hard so that you can make a lot of money no matter what you do.

3. Why does Aunt Victoria have to be my Facebook friend? Don't you trust me?
   a. I think that you are old enough to have a Facebook page. But you also need an adult whom I know and trust to check in.
   b. If you are being responsible it doesn't matter if she is your friend. Why are you concerned?
   c. Do you want me to list all the irresponsible things that you have done this week?
   d. Facebook is full of wackos. I trust you, just not everyone else.

4. I never see Julia at church anymore. She doesn't talk to me in school either.

   a. I know how much you looked up to Julia in youth group. She is a senior now. Maybe she is very busy with college applications, work, and school.

   b. When teenagers get older, church or talking to younger kids isn't cool anymore.

   c. Why don't you send her an e-mail or text to let her know what's happening in youth group and invite her to the next meeting?

   d. Julia has obviously moved on from church and your friendship. You need to do the same.

5. What's the big deal if his parents weren't home? We only watched a movie.

   a. As long as the movie wasn't rated R, that's fine.

   b. Our family rule is that you're not allowed at anyone's house at night when parents aren't home. Our rules are to keep you and your friends safe.

   c. Oh, right. All you did was watch a movie. I know that routine.

   d. What could you have done when you realized his parent's weren't home? (Wait for answer.) Maybe you could have called and watched the movie here?

6. Even if you limit phone minutes, that doesn't change that Jeremy and I are meant to be together forever.

   a. You and Jeremy are a good couple. But, like all relationships, you need to balance it with the time you spend on things like schoolwork, family, church, and other friendships. Until we see that, phone time is limited.

   b. I'd ban you from talking to all boys if I could.

   c. Together forever? You seriously won't last the summer.

   d. You and Jeremy? This is about being responsible and not going over on your minutes. You owe an extra $50 this month. What is your plan for paying the bill?

Answers: 1: a, d; 2: b, c; 3: a, b; 4: a, c; 5: b, d; 6: a, d

Growing and Changing

Middle adolescence is not a long period of time in one's life, but it can seem like an eternity for high schoolers. This is true partly because egocentrism is at its peak in middle adolescence. One is not only figuring out what they want to be (career) but who they want to be in the world. The physical body goes from being a child to being an adult while social responsibilities and freedoms lag slowly behind. This period of life is tough in a very different way than being a child or an adult will ever be. Being prepared for the physical changes and practice at forming healthy relationships can make the bumpy ride of middle adolescence a bit smoother.

Physical Development

When teens begin high school, many of them are in the midst of puberty, others may already appear to have moved through the physical changes, and others are just starting to recognize small changes. By the end of high school most everyone is around the same point. The girls have reached menarche, and the boys, spermarche (for more information refer to physical development in the Tween chapter). Secondary sex characteristics are fully developed, and hormonal fluctuations are settling into patterns. The body is still changing and developing, but most teens have a better sense of what their "final" young adult body will look like. Consequentially, teens have greater control over their body and are less awkward. Some become accomplished dancers, basketball players, swimmers, skateboarders, and so on. They are still preoccupied with their appearance, but they take full responsibility for changing hygiene needs, as well as style. As high school progresses, teens have a way of settling into how they "carry" themselves. In most cases this reflects their growing comfort with their body (body image) and the body coming to some sort of oasis in its development.

In other cases, body image can become a significant issue for teens. Eating disorders for both teen girls and boys are on the rise. For all the positive lessons and media messages about being unique and loving one's self, there are hundreds more that project an unattainable standard for physical appearance. Issues related to depression, eating problems, and early sexual behaviors are associated with poor body image. The teenage years are a critical time to support positive body image for all kids through unsolicited supportive comments, encouraging exercise, and supporting healthy eating.

Most teenagers (even at fourteen years old) are aware that they are sexual people. At this stage they have experienced feelings of attraction, possibly explored their own bodies, and engaged in some of their first sexual behaviors. Some teenagers do not engage in any sexual behaviors and others may choose to express their sexuality in ways that include sexual intercourse. Many high school students engage in a wide variety of sexual behaviors, including outercourse such as kissing, heavy touching, and mutual masturbation, and intercourse such as oral sex, anal sex, and vaginal sex. The Youth Risk Behavior Survey for 2009 reports that about 30 percent of U.S. ninth graders have had sexual intercourse. The numbers go up generally by about 10 percent for each year of high school—40 percent in tenth grade, 50 percent in eleventh grade, and a little over 60 percent by senior year.[1] The statistics represent those who have ever had intercourse where intercourse is defined as penile-vaginal intercourse. The numbers are slightly higher for males than females until senior year where it evens out or more females than males are engaging in sexual intercourse. There are also racial differences. African American and Latino youth are slightly higher than the national average. White and multiple race youth are very close to the national average, and Asian youth are generally below average by ten to fifteen percentage points. Every year the numbers fluctuate slightly, but the trends stay the same. Some teenagers are having "sex," while others are not.

Teenagers need information on contraception and STI protection. Even if they do not plan to have sexual intercourse, almost all will at some point in their lives. And it will most likely be in the near future. A survey of twenty- to twenty-four-year-olds reported that over eight out of ten have engaged in vaginal sexual intercourse.[2] Teenagers, male and female, should be able to clearly explain pregnancy and reproduction. An understanding of how reproduction occurs is key to effective use of contraception. You can't prevent something if you aren't quite sure how it happens in the first place. Teen pregnancy and birth rates, in general, have been decreasing over the past few decades across racial and ethnic groups.[3] Yet there are still teens who will become pregnant and have to make very difficult and potentially life-changing decisions as a result. In many cases, parents can be extremely disappointed or even angry when a daughter or son seeks help with an unintended pregnancy. What a parent can offer, and is needed most, is the response of God's forgiving love, openness to the best decision for those involved, and support from or access to other professionals. There are additional resources at the end of this book for families and teens facing an unintended pregnancy.

Use of Alcohol or Drugs before Sex

Approximately 20 percent of teens report using drugs or alcohol prior to engaging in sexual intercourse. Males are more likely, as are white and mixed-race teens. Thankfully, use of drugs and alcohol prior to intercourse is less likely when one is a senior. Unfortunately, that means a disproportionate number of freshman are engaging in sexual intercourse when using drugs and alcohol, which can impair their judgment at minimum, reduce effectiveness of protection use, and lead to acquaintance rape in the worst scenarios.

Talking with teens about use of drugs and alcohol is important. Talking with them about using drugs and alcohol while making sexual decisions is absolutely imperative.

Teens should also know how HIV and other STIs are transmitted. Again, the same logic applies. If a teen does not know that someone can have an STI without showing any symptoms, a teen might conclude, "I don't see any warts or puss filled bumps, like the horrific pictures they showed me in class. This person doesn't have an STI." In fact, it is very common for someone to have an STI and not have any visible symptoms. It is also common for teens to think that STIs can be transmitted only through vaginal intercourse instead of through oral or anal sex. There is no need to worry that providing information will cause teens to engage in sexual behaviors, especially if parents share accurate information in the values framework of safety and empowerment, not permission.

Q&A

Teen: **Can you get an STI from oral sex?**

Parent: Yes, people can get STIs from oral sex. Someone can have an STI without showing any symptoms. That's why it is important to use a condom for a boy and a dental dam (small stretchable sheet of latex) for a girl during oral sex. Using safer sex practices shows that you care about the other person and want you both to be safe. Remember, oral sex is sex and shouldn't just be rushed into.

Teenagers can also begin to discuss the more abstract consequences related to sexual intercourse outside of pregnancy and STI transmission. As youth progress through high school their brains are changing. These changes allow them to move from concrete thinking to more abstract thinking. This development deepens their ability to plan for the future and understand the future consequences of their actions. Cognitive maturity is central to decision making related to sexual behaviors. Because teens are still mostly concrete thinkers, they may be limited in their ability to fully articulate values, negotiate with a sexual partner, and obtain contraception. As well, cognitive ability is often determinant of one's capacity for empathy, the ability to appreciate another person's situation and perspective. Thus, cognitive development—movement from concrete to abstract thinking—helps youth begin to see how they fit within the larger world, how their actions affect others positively and negatively, and how another person perceives their actions regardless of intent.

The ability to plan for the future also means that teens learn to make decisions based on the knowledge that they have and to find out more information prior to making a decision. Finding accurate and reliable information about sexual relationships and behaviors on the Internet can be like finding a needle in a haystack, and in the process your teen might have to weed through a number of sexualized and/or pornographic images. By high school, teens understand the role media plays in sexualization, but that doesn't always mean that they have a sense of what's appropriate and what's not. They still need guidance and restrictions placed on their use of media— TV, music, movies, phones, and the Internet. (Find helpful tips and resources in the additional resources section.) Parents might also consider bookmarking helpful and trusted Web sites on the main home computer and suggest that the child look at them.

Q&A

Teen: **What's the big deal about sex?**

Parent: Sexual intercourse is one of the most intimate ways that God gave us to share our bodies and express to someone that we love them. I know that TV and songs make it seem like it is just for fun or doesn't mean anything. But that's not real life. Having sexual intercourse with someone is a big decision that takes planning and communication so that it can be as special and enjoyable as possible.

High school youth may point out that kids their age in developing countries or previous times in this country were engaging in sexual intercourse and had families at their age. While that is true, and the entire society hoped and expected that from them, those teens were generally in a social structure where they had married and could take care of a child. Various reasons exist for why it is best to wait to have sexual intercourse until after high school. For example, a teen might appreciate how sexual behaviors, and intercourse in particular, are physically pleasurable and may deepen the emotional connection between two people. But they may ignore that intercourse may also increase their stress level and cause them to hide feelings from each other. Or teens will talk about the fiscal and educational ramifications if one were to become pregnant, but not be concerned about HIV prevention. In other words, teens do weigh the pros and cons of decisions, but they overestimate the benefits of the pros and are often devastated by the negative, unexpected consequences.

The conversation about waiting to engage in mature sexual behaviors does not need to be a fight or even an absolute ban! In the end, your child will make their decision based on all the information they have until this stage. You can encourage them to wait and give them your further reasons. You might tell them what you mean by being ready for sexual intercourse. Ready, from my perspective, includes that a teen couple has

+ tried lots of other mutually pleasurable sexual behaviors that don't have the same risk for disease and pregnancy;
+ talked about the sexual behaviors each has engaged in with other partners and have been tested for STIs and HIV if warranted;
+ shared how sexual intercourse may change physical and emotional aspects of the relationship for the better and for the worse;
+ together, told a trusted adult that they are going to have sexual intercourse and what protection they plan to use;
+ and finally, listened to the trusted adult's advice.

Doing each of these above suggestions shows that the couple knows each other's bodies well, are comfortable talking about sexual behaviors with each other and with other adults, have spent a significant amount of time together, and have thought through future consequences—positive and negative. As parents, it is important to keep in mind that many adults don't take the time to move through the bulleted steps above. There are adults who are not sexually healthy and who do not make choices based on Christian values of love, respect, honesty, pleasure, trust, and shared commitment undergirding the "ready" steps listed above. My hope is not that teens become like *just any* adult, but that they become sexually healthy adults who live out sexual relationships based on their Christian values.

Relational Development

Adolescence is a long process of figuring out who *I* am. Recent studies suggest that adolescence is getting longer as young adults stay in school longer for more education, put off long-term committed relationships, and live more transient lives, having to move multiple times for work (if they can find a job). Over time, one's identity becomes clearer as teens develop a sense of autonomy and self-sufficiency while still living within family, school, and church structures.

Most parents try very hard to establish open and loving communication with their teen while still maintaining their role as parent. In seeking autonomy it can be difficult for adolescents as they begin a variety of new interpersonal relationships while maintaining established family ones. This process of independence can be exciting, painful, anxiety-provoking, and difficult for all parties—parents and children alike. Some teens are able to handle the nuances and balance needed to start separating from the family and moving onto the next stage in life. Other teens can become rude and disrespectful to their parents, latching on to friends or a romantic partner in an attempt to completely sever parental ties. Most teens fall somewhere in the middle. In other words, finding a balanced way to maintain relationships while forming new ones is a developmental skill; and it is one that many of us spend our lives working to accomplish.

Hopefully, parents have set a good example for how to maintain multiple relationships and kids have walked through making new friends and leaving old ones. These two experiences provide examples for how to start and end relationships in healthy ways. Even with the best-laid plans, teens will struggle and push against parents and family most severely. Parents should point out when they see their teen pushing against them and favoring friends or dismissing one friend for a new group. These observations do not need to be judgmental unless teens are being intentionally hurtful or disrespectful, but they should point out the discontinuity. Most teens just don't notice what they are doing. For example, imagine that a teen blows up over the fact that she is being forced to attend a family gathering rather than go to a friend's house. A parent might say, "This is a family commitment, and as a member of the family you are coming. We aren't asking you to pick your family over your friends. You can be part of the family and still have great friends. You just have to be able to give time to both. That's part of showing respect and balancing relationships."

Dating. Teens may also end other friendships when they become romantically involved with one person (often part of the crush phase). Middle adolescents often experience the classic "teenage love." This is not to be diminished or ridiculed. By age eighteen, more than eight in ten teens report having been in a relationship.[4] Again, every teen is different, and some may not date at all, while others date multiple people during high school and college years. There is no "normal" way to progress through romantic relationships. There are only more or less typical patterns of dating. Even without dating, first loves and crushes are a typical part of adolescent development. Unfortunately, many adults do not take these feelings or relationships very seriously. They may even dismiss them as "puppy love." Yet teens understand their relationships very differently, and adults should as well. Often, the unrealistic expectations that adolescents place on these relationships can be heartbreaking and cause depression. This underscores the seriousness that teens place on these relationships, and parents should not dismiss these strong emotions since unchecked depression can lead to use of negative coping mechanisms like decline in self-image and, in severe cases, even suicide. Navigating how to start dating and dealing with breaking up can teach teens coping skills and resiliency. That doesn't make breaking up any easier, but most youth will learn something in the process and be able to apply that to other relationships.

The emotional rollercoaster of dating can be difficult to deal with as a teen. Even so, intimate relationships can contribute to healthy emotional development. Learning to share feelings and become vulnerable in a relationship takes a great deal of trust. Vulnerability, in healthy relationships, is reciprocal and thus requires respect and care from the other person. It also helps teens know how to put healthy relationship values like honesty, respect, mutual pleasure, shared decision making, and trust into practice. As teens gain independence from close family relationships, these new partnerships help them test ways of cultivating companionship and trust. Dating relationships are a practical—and enjoyable—way to learn how to balance emotions, hone personal skills, and learn more about the person one wants to be through sharing and reflection. Many lesbian and gay teens do not have the opportunity to date their own sex during middle and high school, and so they may end up working through similar relationship issues in college.

By late adolescence, most teens have settled into a more realistic sense of what is expected of self and others in relationships. The quality and character of early romantic and dating relationships begins to shape personal understandings of romance; intimacy; sexuality; and, perhaps most important, self-esteem. Certainly, keeping a relationship with God through prayer encourages reflection and can strengthen other relationships as one becomes more confident and secure in her- or himself.

Abstinence-Only-Until-Marriage: Is That the Best Message?

Abstinence-only-until-marriage education and pledges (sometimes called purity culture or pledges) do not prevent teens from engaging in sexual intercourse prior to marriage. Research on virginity pledges show that in early and middle adolescence, pledging delays the average time of first sexual intercourse by only eighteen months; it does not delay intercourse until marriage. Moreover, pledging works best when the pledgers are a small or minority identity group (less than one-third) of a school or class. Those teens in the study who broke the pledge were one-third less likely to use contraception than teens who had not pledged.[5] Abstinence-only education also promotes gender stereotypes and leads youth to define abstinence as only avoiding (vaginal) intercourse. Thus, many teens believe any other sexual behaviors are permissible.[6]

The fact remains that from 1954 to 2003, trends in premarital sex have seen no great change. By age twenty, 75 percent of all U.S. men and women have had premarital sex and by age forty-four, 95 percent of people have had premarital sex. Clearly, virginity pledges and abstinence-only-until-marriage are not the best messages to delaying sexual intercourse. What's the alternative? Research shows that teens delay sexual intercourse when they have

+ a supportive environment,
+ open communication with parents and influential adults,
+ positive self-identity or esteem,
+ pro-social activities (church, sports, hobbies),
+ and a sense that one has future prospects of success after high school.[7]

Parents can promote waiting in high school while also talking openly about contraception, STI prevention, and mutual pleasure in sexual relationships, as well as what Christian values and qualities make for a healthy sexual relationship.

Intimacy and Sexual Behaviors. Balancing intimacy and sexual behaviors in relationships takes practice for teens. Intimacy is developed through relationships and responds to our body's need for touch. Pleasurable touch communicates warmth, love, care, and grows intimacy. A minister friend of mine is fond of saying, "We were created as much for delight as for duty." God did not make a mistake when creating us or the rest of creation. We are to delight in love, in the beauty around us, and in ourselves. When it comes to sexuality, most Christian messages err on the side of duty over delight. There is a general fear that too much delight moves us further away from God. But this is based on a misinterpretation of *pleasure* as whatever feels good regardless of other people and that sexual desire is a *slippery slope.*

Sexuality education materials focused on abstinence often give teens the message that if they begin kissing or touching, they won't stop! Sexual desire and sexual behaviors are often portrayed as uncontrollable and gender biased. For example, girls are cautioned to not tempt boys because boys can't resist. Sexual desires can be strong, but each of us is always responsible for our actions and just because we feel a certain way doesn't mean we need to act on it. We know that people can stop sexual behaviors at any time—ever have your child knock at your bedroom door unexpectedly when you and your partner were just about to engage in intercourse? A sexually healthy adult knows the difference between sexual feelings and behaviors as well as appropriate times and locations for intimate sexual expression. This message helps teens understand that sexual behaviors are not inevitable—as in, we just kissed, so next time we have to touch, then next time we should have oral sex. We can decide to engage in a behavior one day and stop the next if it doesn't feel right for the relationship or for that moment.

An open discussion about pleasurable options outside of intercourse encourages teens to set positive limits, like we can kiss, but no touching, or we can touch each other, but no forms of intercourse. There are many pleasure behaviors that are appropriate and safe for teens in a romantic relationship. Engagement in a variety of pleasurable sexual behaviors can promote communication, encourage learning about one's own body, and contribute to teens delaying intercourse.

> **Q&A**
>
> *Teen:* **Please don't get mad. Brianna and I had sex a few times. We always use protection. It was fine, but I don't think I want to anymore.**
>
> *Parent:* I'm really thankful that you came to me. I'm also glad that you used protection. I do think you are too young to have sex. Like any other sexual behavior, you do not have to do it if you don't want and just because you did it once, or a bunch of times, doesn't mean that you have to do it again. Do you want to talk about how you might tell Brianna how you are feeling?

Teaching about sexual pleasure can and should happen at the same time as lessons about responsibility and care for self and others. We use the euphemism "making love" for sexual intercourse because intimate and pleasurable expressions are part of living out the love commandment—loving God and our neighbor as ourselves. Without the openness to talk about sexual pleasure and intimacy, teens will not have the vocabulary or experiences that will allow them to communicate healthy limits for sexual behaviors, to know their own bodies and orientations, or to be comfortable with and empowered by their relationship with God.

Sexual Orientation and Gender Identity. Acceptance of one's sexual identity is often more difficult than many parents understand. Most teens' bodies have not finished growing and changing. Learning to love our bodies through transitions can be difficult and will be something that is ever present (think of middle-age weight gain, menopause, or graying and loss of hair). Teens may also still be exploring feelings of attraction. For example, a freshman girl may take a boy to dances or even date him for a period of time, but by senior year she may have come to know her sexual orientation as lesbian or bisexual and be in a same-sex relationship. That is to say, dating or sexual behaviors do not determine one's sexual orientation forever. Yet, by the end of high school, most teens have a fairly settled idea of their gender identity and sexual orientation.

Teens are often their own worst critic, compounded by cultural messages and peer pressure. Many boys and girls experience gender and sexuality-based bullying and ridicule—making fun of a girl for small breasts or being overweight and making fun of a boy for being too skinny or nonathletic. Many of us might think of this as "the usual" immature high school hazing. However, experience of bullying and suicide attempts are higher for bisexual or questioning teens and significantly higher for gay and lesbian teens.[8]

In some cases, Christian teachings are used to bully and degrade gay, lesbian, bisexual, and questioning teens. From a Christian perspective, when one is taught that sexuality is a good gift, it should not just be some people's sexuality. God created each of us and our sexuality. Christian communities and parents need to recognize that about 12 percent of youth in faith communities self-identify as lesbian, gay, or bisexual.[9] Only 36 percent reported that a youth worker, adviser, or other adult leader in the church knows of their orientation. The majority of youth feel uncomfortable sharing this information about a core element of their sexual identity. Most denominations preach inclusivity of people if not behaviors; however, teaching *homosexuality is wrong* can send a mixed message that the *person* has some inherent flaw or sinfulness. As one Missouri Synod Lutheran pastor in the "Teenage Sexuality and Religion Research Project" responded,

> I never thought before about the possibility that we actually had homosexual teenagers who were active in our church. But with a youth group with forty kids in it, we have to have some who are homosexual or at least who are

struggling with identity issues. As negative as I've been about homosexuality, none of them would ever approach me. That has to change. We've got to find some more compassionate ways to respond to these young people.[10]

Many gay, lesbian, or questioning teens experience discrimination and feel (or know) that parents and churches believe homosexuals are immoral or even less than human because of their orientation. Even in the most progressive families, youth still need to hear and see that all loving, committed, and respectful relationships are honored and blessed. The gender of the two people is not what makes a relationship healthy. The way they treat one another with respect is what makes a relationship healthy.

Parents often make assumptions when talking with teens. It can be difficult to keep open lines of communication about the possibilities for gender identity and sexual orientation. In a conversation with a high school girl who was telling me about prom, I realized halfway through the conversation that I had used the pronoun "he" for her date even though she hadn't. I stopped for a second, and said, "That was really presumptuous of me. I don't even know who your date is. I just made up a guy who looks like a fairy-tale prince. I don't even know your date's gender or your orientation. Sorry." She laughed at me and said, "He wasn't a prince, but he looked pretty good." My intention was to joke about gender roles, apologize, and give her a chance to correct me all at the same time. No matter how vigilant parents are, there is no doubt that heterosexual and sexist stereotypes will pop up in conversations and questions. Parents who take the time to correct these assumptions and respond inclusively set an example that outshines the occasional slipup.

Faith Development

Teenage faith development is often a very personal journey. Many teens may begin to believe that faith is only an individual experience. This can be detrimental for their commitment to organized religion. Christian values and beliefs are collective, and there is an expectation for community. Jesus called disciples and engaged them in rituals and acts of ministry together. He had an expectation that their faith, if it was what he was teaching, would need communal celebration and require acts of care for others. Christian faith development is more than figuring out how religion personally works for you. For example, love of neighbor requires Christians to serve and support others as they would themselves. This is not just through charity but through working for just causes, reaching out to fellow congregants, and worshiping together in community.

In order to test out the faith tradition, teens will go through a process of challenging, questioning, and eventually owning faith commitments. When challenging faith commitments, teens often ask why do we have to pray the same prayer at the same time every service, why do we read the Bible if we know lots of it didn't really happen, why must we pray when nothing ever changes in the world, and so on. Hopefully within the context of a confirmation or Sunday school program, they have the opportunity to question the purpose and meaning of the beliefs and practices. In this process, teens are invited to assess and learn the history of teachings in Christian tradition, Scripture, liturgy, and their denomination.

Throughout the process of questioning, many teens begin to reassemble their faith commitments and determine how relevant and meaningful the information gathered is on both a philosophical level (does it make sense) and a personal level (do I believe what is impossible to prove). In most cases, a clearer picture of their faith emerges and teens choose to make it their own—claim the faith commitments and begin to live by them through individual actions and community commitments. At that point, teens develop a sense that others need to live by these commitments too because they carry truth, not just personal opinion.

When challenging and questioning, many teens try on another faith tradition, maybe even a friend's tradition, similar to how they try on different identities (preppy, goth, sporty, musician, artist, and so forth). Teens are often interested in multifaith projects. The interfaith engagement often ends up teaching them as much about their own faith and ability to talk about commitments to it as it does helping them understand a new faith tradition.

Remember, adolescence is a long process of determining *who I am*. In a sense, the faith journey asks teens to begin figuring out how *who I am* (self-identity) relates to the *I am* (or God). In other words, their faith story has to become consistent with their view of self. Teens tend to connect with the prophets and disciples. Similarly, teens struggle with following God's calling and what people will think of them if they are open about their beliefs. The prophets and disciples also had a difficult time immediately figuring out what God asked of them, and they definitely got into some trouble along the way that ultimately God forgave. Indecision, concern for peer group, and fumbling for clarity are common experiences for teens (most of us really) that find resonance even with some of the most prominent figures in the Jewish and Christian Scriptures. Examples like the books of Daniel, Ruth, and Jonah; Deborah (Judges 4 and 5); doubting Thomas (John 20:19-29); wavering Peter (Mark 14:66-72); or the Syrophoenician woman (Mark 7:25-30, Matt. 15:21-28) make for great lessons to talk about intimacy with God, self-identity, and peer pressure.

Q&A

Teen: **Confirmation is going to be stupid. I didn't like Sunday school. Do I have to go?**

Parent: Whether you want to get confirmed or not is your choice. But as your parent(s), we don't want you to make that decision until you have the information and experiences needed to make an informed, mature choice. Going to confirmation classes, having a mentor, and participating in the service projects will give you that. So, yes, you are going to participate in the confirmation program.

During the teen years, many Christian churches have programs that help teens transition into adulthood. Some churches have youth join the congregation as an adult member. Some have confirmation classes where kids learn to articulate their faith. Some practice adult baptism, which requires a decision made by the person. The structure of education around this spiritual journey is diverse but usually includes spending many evenings at church taking apart the faith tradition, questioning it, and rebuilding it into something they understand and will choose to accept or not. Youth are usually asked during the process to write a credo or faith statement in order to put to paper what their beliefs are. This is a concrete educational exercise for youth that highlights the steps of moral development and ownership of one's faith beliefs. In this process, parents, youth leaders, and mentors in the church serve as guides and conversation partners. The credo could turn into a *personal myth* if it does not engage a larger framework of religious tradition and church. That doesn't mean that the credo can't challenge current beliefs and practices. However, it is important to learn to articulate one's faith within the context of a community to ensure that we are accountable to more than just ourselves, therefore pushing against the individualism of adolescent development and toward a richer understanding of faith as bound to community and God.

Service projects are usually part of teen youth group activities and confirmation programs. Like elementary and middle school kids, teens learn a great deal about faith commitments through the work of service. As teenagers, youth also understand the larger social issues that cause oppression like poverty, racism, sexism, and health disparities. Service projects often become charity events. When done in conjunction with learning Scripture and theology, service projects can be transformed into service learning and deeply influence a teen's faith journey. It is a living example of why faith is not just an individual thing, but it calls us to respond to God's calling and Jesus' example of justice. If we all did what we feel is right for us, there would be few collective movements to end the injustices that astound teens in service learning. They not only intellectually get it, but they see the need for significant change that will take many hands and a collective commitment.

Connecting Our Faith and Sexuality Education

As teens move into adult roles in the congregation, they need participatory, educational, and reflective opportunities that make connections between their faith and healthy sexual development. The first and most significant factor for teens is active participation in a faith community. The second is education about the sexuality and relationship teachings within a Christian context. And lastly, teens need examples of how real people live out their faith in relationship.

Research shows that a significant contributor to healthy sexual development and waiting to have intercourse is active participation in a faith community. This means teens who say religion is very important and who regularly attend church are less likely to engage in sexual intercourse.[11] Religious commitment is also correlated with whether a teen has engaged in sexual or intimate activities *other* than vaginal intercourse for both teen girls and boys. The more importance a teenager places on religion, the less likely he or she is to have engaged in oral sex for example.[12] While the rate of sexual intercourse for religiously involved youth is lower, their engagement in oral sex may be surprising to parents, religious leaders, and teachers. Some researchers suggest that teens substitute oral sex for vaginal intercourse as a "loop hole" to avoid losing their virginity or breaking family and church rules. Recent research finds that teens often opt for oral sex to "safeguard their future schooling plans, career trajectories, and life chances" not as a ploy to maintain "technical virginity."[13] Unfortunately, many of the teens do not see oral sex as involving any danger of transmission for HIV/AIDS or other STIs.[14]

Teens who wait to engage in sexual behaviors say that their congregation's teachings and/or Scripture influence their decision making. Teens understand that there are inconsistencies within

Scripture and how current Christian theology interprets sexual relationships and teachings from Scripture differently than it did in previous generations. For example, much of the gender inequality and even violence that happens to young women is no longer tolerated by or practiced in most Christian communities.

In their transition from concrete to abstract thinking, teens can differentiate relationship values that are seen throughout Scripture and resist picking and choosing one isolated text over and against another. They, like most churches, believe the Christian tradition supports gender equality and women's equal participation in faith communities versus the inequality set forth by some of the marriage practices and texts, such as having many wives or concubines in the Hebrew Scriptures (1 Cor. 11:3; Eph. 5:22–24; Titus 2:5; 1 Pet. 3:1–2) or laws about rape and incest (Gen. 19:30–36; Deut. 21 and 22; Num. 31:17–18; 2 Kgs. 13). Similarly, teens have a sophisticated (and persistent) sense of questioning that often leads them to reject conservative interpretations of sexual orientation. In fact, current teens and young adults "frequently mentioned being anti-gay and judgmental as key attributes that turned off younger adults about contemporary churches."[15]

Sexuality education for teens should expand to include relationship education in a more formal sense. Teens in the survey discussed above said adults who work with them portray sex in a healthy and positive way. For teens who are dealing with sexual attraction, parents can address how faith relates to sexual pleasure. There are many scriptural examples that support sexual pleasure as part of our createdness and our religious experience. After finding out that Sarah is going to conceive a baby with Abraham, she "laughed to herself, saying, 'After I have grown old, and my husband is old, shall I have pleasure?'" (Gen. 18:12). She knows that she will have sexual intercourse to have a baby. The Song of Songs is an entire book of Scripture dedicated to sexual pleasure and love. The story of Mary washing Jesus' feet with oil and her hair shows that Jesus engages in intimate and sensual behavior. In fact, most of the church's rituals include sensuality and intimacy in an affirmation of our bodies. Laying on of hands in blessing, lighting candles, and anointing with oil and water are all ways that Christians experience ritual and affirm sensuality as a healthy expression of sexuality.

Q&A

Teen: **Marriage is so overrated. I don't understand why everyone is arguing about it.**

Parent: There is a difference between people arguing about the state's marriage practice, which is a legal piece of paper, and what churches believe. In our Christian faith, marriage is a declaration not just of love but of your commitment to be partners with each other through a lifetime of joys and troubles. The whole community blesses it, and God is part of that. Some people want to say that any man or woman can make a marriage. But we believe that it isn't about gender; marriage is about creating a healthy relationship and family. Any two people can do that, but it takes a lot of work and commitment. (Further explanation based on family situation might be needed. Such as, sometimes people can't always keep those promises; that's why we have divorce.)

Hopefully, relationship education has been taking place throughout a child's life in church school. At this point, it can be more directly applied to issues of romantic relationships, dating, and marriage. The love commandment suggests a balance between God, self, and other is needed in relationships. For many teens, including God in their romantic relationships seems odd. I usually ask youth to draw a scale like they use in chemistry class—balance in the middle, weighing plates on the left and right sides. I have them put God on one side and boy/girlfriend on the other. Then I ask them to write things that they could do that would make sure the balance stayed even, meaning God didn't get completely left out and drop down to zero while the boy/girlfriend side rises up to 100. They often look at me like I'm crazy at first. Then someone sheepishly offers a suggestion. "I don't know, maybe pray together or for each other and your relationship." Then the answers start coming: go to church together, do service projects, attend each other's youth group if you aren't from the same church, talk about your beliefs, and so on. Doing these things requires a level of intimacy and sharing of one's faith. That can be scary, awkward, or just seem goofy in our very secular lives.

Teens tend to have an overly romanticized view of love. Clarifying the Christian tradition's notion of love as incorporating more than intimate sexual acts is one helpful way to define what leads to a healthy versus unhealthy relationship. Wedding ceremonies are the place we most often hear the apostle Paul's description of love (1 Cor. 13:1–8). There is a good reason for this. Relationships that are healthy need a mix of healthy characteristics to last. Paul's description of love enumerates a variety of characteristics that undergird healthy relationships as well as naming those that do not. The letter includes a movement from childhood to adulthood as a way the author learned that love is the highest value in relationships. This love is not a mushy head-over-heals love, though it may include that. The list of what love is (patient, kind, truthful, believing, hoping, and enduring) and what love is not (envious, boastful, arrogant, rude, selfish, irritable, resentful) provides a guideline for how youth can assess their relationships.

From what we know, adolescent developmental tendencies are at times in opposition to what Paul describes as the characteristics of love. Egocentrism, desire to fit in and follow the group, fleeting crushes, and difficulty seeing another person's perspective resemble the negative characteristics on Paul's list. Remember, teens are in a process of developing into confident, relational, committed, and empathetic individuals. They will get there with a bit of help. Until then, playing on the strengths of their developmental stage will help them begin building healthy relationships earlier.

Parents can create opportunities for teens to clarify their values and understand why Paul (and many Christians) define love and healthy relationships as they do. Teens have to test out those characteristics and see if they can identify them within their friendships and current romantic relationships. Most importantly, teens have to want to make these values their own! Ownership of values and beliefs (not being told "they have to") leads to youth living them out in their everyday lives.

Parents and youth leaders can help keep teens on the path to balanced relationships by setting limits on dating and keeping open communication (even when teens think they don't need parent relationships anymore). For example, parents and youth leaders should encourage dating age-appropriate partners (usually less than a two-year difference). They can also provide the supervision that teens need. When teens are allowed to be alone in rooms with doors closed or no one home, they are more likely to engage in risky behaviors. Privacy is important to building relationships, but teens should know that time alone in the family room or on a retreat is likely to be interrupted by other family members or the youth leader. Similarly in early dating stages, going out with a group of friends or to a public place means that you have to interact with everyone and also offers less time for one-on-one sexual behaviors. In fact, practices such as these model a balance between romantic relationships, family relationships, and friendships.

Teens also need nonparent mentors in their faith journey. In most congregations, it is common to find a sponsor for a teen who is going through confirmation. These people serve as role models by sharing their faith journey, commitment to the congregation, and generosity of time with the teen. As teens participate in more church programs, they form relationships with more adults who become role models—the choir director, the hospitality committee members, the social action team. Teens observe how they connect their faith values to their relationships and life choices. Parents can encourage this kind of observation by pointing it out once in a while. For example, a parent might say, "Anthony and Kendra are so active and involved in their coleadership of the social action committee. Their relationship is close to what I think Jesus means by living out love for self, other, and God in our lives." Or, "Jennifer and Monica really make participation in church a central part of their relationship. It's incredible how their son Alex is following their example."

Not all examples of relationships are going to be positive. Teens need space to talk about bad relationships or peer pressure that goes against their values in decision making. No one is perfect, and forgiveness is abundant; that is part of the Christian faith tradition as well. Given the right mix of participation, education, and reflection, teens will develop a deep sense of how faith is part of their identity and how that fits with a healthy sexuality.

TEACHABLE MESSAGES AND MOMENTS

I AM (God) is part of who I am (self-identity).

+ Know and accept gender identity and sexual orientation.
+ Affirm that God created sexuality, sexual pleasure is good, and we are in control of behaviors.
+ Understand that exploring sexual behaviors is typical and should reflect relationship values.
+ Know about and, if needed, use safer sex practices like contraception and STI prevention methods.

Love commandment is the golden rule for all relationships.

+ Name and identify the components of healthy and unhealthy relationships.
+ Intentionally create time for relationships.
+ Teach that decisions have consequences—grown-ups weigh them and then act; they take responsibility for behavior.
+ Practice positive limit setting by determining what behaviors are appropriate based on age, length of relationship, and knowledge of each other.
+ Recognize the role that the media plays in crafting views about sex and sexuality.

Journeys require guides and mentors.

+ Know that parents are still needed, even when not appreciated.
+ Learn about intimate, loving, long-term relationships through observation and marriage/parenting education.
+ Talk through future planning without over-determining decisions (marriage, college, what you want to be).
+ Keep up with faith rituals and traditions—confirmation is a start not an end.
+ Be a part of romantic relationships and friendships to show interest in your teen's life.
+ Set parameters on technology and check up.

REFLECTIONS

Write down a few things you learned from this chapter, some examples from your own life that reflect the teachable messages, or a reminder of something you want to do or say.

Notes

Chapter 1: Five Common Myths

1. For detailed information and research related to this myth, see Trisha Mueller, Lorrie E. Gavin, and Aniket Kulkarni, "The Association between Sex Education and Youth's Engagement in Sexual Intercourse, Age at First Intercourse, and Birth Control Use at First Sex," *Journal of Adolescent Health* 42 (2008): 89–96; Douglas Kirby, *Emerging Answers: Research Findings on Programs to Reduce Teen Pregnancy* (Washington, DC: National Campaign to Prevent Teen Pregnancy, 2001).

Chapter 5: What's Changed Since I Was a Kid?

1. See the recent article from the American Psychological Association, "Task Force on the Sexualization of Girls, Report" (2010), http://www.apa.org/pi/women/programs/girls/report-full.pdf.
2. Dale Kunke, Keren Eyal, Keli Finnerty, Erica Biely, and Edward Donnerstein, "Sex on TV 4," A Kaiser Family Foundation Report (November 2005), http://kff.org/other/event/sex-on-tv-4/.

3. Guttmacher Institute, "Facts on American Teens' Sources of Information about Sex" (December 2011), http://www.guttmacher .org/pubs/FB-Teen-Sex-Ed.html#16.

4. Lawrence B. Finer and Jesse M. Philbin, "Sexual Initiation, Contraceptive Use, and Pregnancy among Young Adolescents," *Pediatrics* (April 2013): 2012-3495, http://pediatrics.aappublications .org/content/early/2013/03/27/peds.2012-3495.

5. National Center for Chronic Disease Prevention and Health Promotion, Division for Adolescent and School Health, "High School Youth Risk Behavior Survey, 2009" (2010), http://apps.nccd.cdc .gov/youthonline.

6. Lawrence B. Finer, "Trends in Premarital Sex in the United States, 1954-2003," *Public Health Reports* 122 (January–Feburary 2007).

7. Casey E. Copen, Anjani Chandra, and Gladys Martinez, "Prevalence and Timing of Oral Sex with Opposite-Sex Partners among Females and Males Aged 15-24 Years: United States, 2007–2010," National Health Statistics Reports, Division of Vital Statistics, no. 56 (2012). Study compares oral sex and vaginal sex behaviors.

8. As early as 2007, *USA Today* was reporting on the trend that gay kids are "coming out" earlier. See Marilyn Elias, "Gay Teens Coming Out Earlier to Peers and Family," *USA Today*, February 11, 2007, http://www.usatoday.com/news/nation/2007-02-07 -gay-teens-cover_x.htm.

9. Stephen T. Russell, Hinda Seif, and Nhan L. Truong, "School Outcomes of Sexual Minority Youth in the United States: Evidence from a National Study," *Journal of Adolescence* 24, no. 1 (February 2001): 111-27.

10. See Mark Regnerus and Jeremy Uecker, *Premarital Sex in America: How Young Americans Meet, Mate, and Think about Marrying* (New York: Oxford University Press, 2011) for a fuller discussion of these trends.

Chapter 7: Birth to Kindergartners (0–5)

1. See Gail Hornor, "Sexual Behavior in Children: Normal or Not?" *Journal of Pediatric Health Care* 18 (2004): 57-64; National

Child Traumatic Stress Network, "Sexual Development and Behavior in Children: Information for Parents & Caregivers" (April 2009), http://nctsn.org/nctsn_assets/pdfs/caring/sexual developmentandbehavior.pdf.

2. New research by Bloom and Wynne was highlighted in Paul Bloom, "Are Babies Moral?" *New York Times Magazine*, May 8, 2010. See also, Paul Bloom, *Descartes' Baby: How the Science of Child Development Explains What Makes Us Human* (New York: Basic Books, 2005).

3. Pamela Cooper-White, "Human Development in Relational and Cultural Context," in *Human Development and Faith: Life-Cycle Stages of Body, Mind, and Soul,* ed. Felicity B. Kelcourse (St. Louis: Chalice Press, 2004), 91–125.

4. See Joyce Ann Mercer, *Welcoming Children: A Practical Theology of Childhood* (St. Louis: Chalice Press, 2005); Karen M. Yust, *Real Kids, Real Faith: Practices for Nurturing Children's Spiritual Lives* (San Francisco: Jossey-Bass, 2004).

Chapter 8: Elementary School Years (6–10)

1. See the helpful chart on sex play to determine if behaviors are harmless or problematic in Debra W. Haffner, *From Diapers to Dating: A Parent's Guide to Raising Sexually Healthy Children* (New York: New Market Press, 2000), 60.

2. Vivian Thompson, "Acculturation and Latency," in *Human Development and Faith: Life-Cycle Stages of Body, Mind, and Soul,* ed. Felicity B. Kelcourse (St. Louis: Chalice Press, 2004), 183–204.

Chapter 9: Middle School Years (11–13)

1. National Center for Chronic Disease Prevention and Health Promotion, Division for Adolescent and School Health, "High School Youth Risk Behavior Survey, 2009" (2010), http://apps.nccd.cdc .gov/youthonline.

2. Statistics from Choose Respect, retrieved from http://www .chooserespect.org/scripts/teens/statistics.asp.

3. Teenage Research Limited, "Teen Relationships Abuse Survey, 2008," http://www.loveisnotabuse.com/statistics.htm.

4. Marin B. Vanoss, et al., "Older Boyfriends and Girlfriends Increase Risk of Sexual Initiation in Young Adolescents," *Journal of Adolescent Health* 27 (2000): 409-18.

5. The National Campaign to Prevent Teen and Unplanned Pregnancy with Cosmogirl.com, "Sex and Tech Survey" (2008), http://www.thenationalcampaign.org/sextech/.

6. Janis Wolak, Kimberly Mitchell, and David Finkelhor, "Unwanted and Wanted Exposure to Online Pornography in a National Sample of Youth Internet Users," *Pediatrics* 119 (2007): 247-57.

7. Jochen Peter and Patti M. Valkenburg, "Adolescents' Exposure to Sexually Explicit Online Material and Recreational Attitudes toward Sex," *Journal of Communication* 56, no. 4 (Dec 2006): 639-60.

8. Ronald Nydam, "Early Adolescence: Venturing toward a Different World" in *Human Development and Faith: Life-Cycle Stages of Body, Mind, and Soul*, ed. Felicity B. Kelcourse (St. Louis: Chalice Press, 2004), 205-22.

Chapter 10: High School Years (14-18)

1. National Center for Chronic Disease Prevention and Health Promotion, Division for Adolescent and School Health, "High School Youth Risk Behavior Survey, 2009" (2010), http://apps.nccd.cdc.gov/youthonline.

2. Casey E. Copen, Anjani Chandra, and Gladys Martinez, "Prevalence and Timing of Oral Sex with Opposite-Sex Partners among Females and Males Aged 15-24 Years: United States, 2007-2010," National Health Statistics Reports, Division of Vital Statistics, no. 56 (2012).

3. See Brady E. Hamilton and Stephanie J. Ventura, "Birth Rates for U.S. Teenagers Reach Historic Lows for All Age and Ethnic Groups," National Center for Health Statistics Data Brief, no. 89 (April 2012), http://www.cdc.gov/nchs/data/databriefs/db89.htm. See also "Facts on Unintended Pregnancy in the United States," In Brief: Fact Sheet of Guttmacher Institute (January 2012), http://www.guttmacher.org/pubs/FB-Unintended-Pregnancy-US.pdf.

4. Sarah Sorensen, "Adolescent Romantic Relationships," ACT

for Youth Center of Excellence, Research Facts and Findings (July 2007), http://www.actforyouth.net/resources/rf/rf_romantic_0707.pdf.

5. Peter S. Bearman and Hannah Brückner, "Promising the Future: Virginity Pledges as They Affect Transition to First Intercourse," *The American Journal of Sociology* 106 (2001): 859–912.

6. Lisa Remez,"Oral Sex among Adolescents: Is It Sex or Is It Abstinence?" *Family Planning Perspectives* 32 (2000): 298–304.

7. Douglas Kirby, "No Easy Answers: Research Findings on Programs to Reduce Teen Pregnancy" (Washington, DC: The National Campaign to Prevent Teen Pregnancy, 1997), 47.

8. Centers for Disease Control and Prevention, "Sexual Identity, Sex of Sexual Contacts, and Health-Risk Behaviors among Students in Grade 9–12: Youth Risk Behavior Surveillance, Selected Sites, United States, 2001-2009," *Morbidity and Mortality Weekly Report,* no. 60 (June 10 2011), http://www.cdc.gov/mmwr/preview/mmwrhtml/ss6007a1.htm.

9. Steve Clapp, *Faith Matters: Teenagers, Religion, and Sexuality* (LifeQuest, 2003), 96.

10. Ibid., 93.

11. Mark D. Regnerus, *Forbidden Fruit: Sex and Religion in the Lives of American Teenagers* (New York: Oxford University Press, 2007), 119–22.

12. Ibid., 163–66.

13. Ibid., 182.

14. Kaiser Family Foundation, "National Survey of Adolescents and Young Adults: Sexual Health Knowledge, Attitudes and Experiences" (May 2003), http://www.kff.org/youthhivstds/3218-index.cfm.

15. Robert P. Jones and Daniel Cox, "Doing Church and Doing Justice: A Portrait of Millennials at Middle Church," Public Religion Research Project (May 2011), http://publicreligion.org/research/2011/05/doing-church-and-doing-justice-a-portrait-of-millennials-at-middle-church.

Additional Resources

Every parent should have a collection of a few good resource books and bookmarked Web sites to turn to for information and advice. Here are a few recommendations.

Resources for Parents

Sexuality Information and Education

Haffner, Debra W. *From Diapers to Dating: A Parent's Guide to Raising Sexually Healthy Children.* New York: New Market, 2000.

———. *Beyond the Big Talk: Every Parent's Guide to Raising Sexually Healthy Teens.* New York: New Market, 2002.

Planned Parenthood Parent Education. http://www.plannedparenthood.org/parents/.

Religious Institute. http://www.religiousinstitute.org/resources. For organizational links to faith-based groups that work on sexuality education, abuse prevention, LGBT issues, and reproductive health.

Roffman, Deborah. *But How'd I Get in There in the First Place? Talking to Your Young Child about Sex.* Cambridge, MA: Perseus, 2002.

Rutgers University. Answer: Sex Ed, Honestly. http://answer.rutgers.edu/.

United Church of Christ. Our Whole Lives. This is a series of sexuality education programs for six age groups: grades K-1, grades 4-6, grades 7-9, grades 10-12, young adults, and adults. There are materials for each age group, including a leader's guide, parent guides for K-1 and 4-6, as well as a supplementary series called Sexuality and Our Faith. http://www.ucc.org/justice/sexuality-education/our-whole-lives.html.

Faith Development

Dykstra, Robert C., Allan Hugh Cole Jr., and Donald Capps. *The Faith and Friendships of Teenage Boys.* Louisville, KY: Westminster John Knox, 2012.

Mercer, Joyce Ann. *Welcoming Children: A Practical Theology of Childhood.* St. Louis: Chalice, 2005.

Parker, Evelyn, ed. *The Sacred Selves of Adolescent Girls: Hard Stories of Race, Class, and Gender.* Eugene, OR: Wipf & Stock Publishers, 2010.

Reid, Kathryn Goering and Ken Hawkley. *Children Together: Teaching Girls and Boys to Value Themselves and Each Other.* Eugene, OR: Wipf & Stock Publishers, 2010.

Yust, Karen Marie. *Real Kids, Real Faith: Practices for Nurturing Children's Spiritual Lives.* San Francisco: Jossey Bass, 2004.

Sexuality and Christianity

Countryman, William. *Dirt, Greed, and Sex: Sexual Ethics in the New Testament and Their Implications for Today.* Rev. ed. Minneapolis: Fortress, 2007.

De La Torre, Miguel. *A Lily among the Thorns: Imagining a New Christian Sexuality.* San Francisco: Jossey Bass, 2007.

Ellison, Marvin. *Making Love Just: Sexual Ethics for Perplexing Times.* Minneapolis: Fortress, 2012.

Farley, Margaret. *Just Love: A Framework for Christian Sexual Ethics.* New York: Continuum, 2006.

Sexual Abuse and Violence Prevention

Centers for Disease Control and Prevention. "Teen Dating Violence." http://www.cdc.gov/ViolencePrevention/intimatepartnerviolence/teen_dating_violence.html.

FaithTrust Institute. http://www.faithtrustinstitute.org. This is a faith-based organization working to end sexual and domestic violence.

Miles, Al. *Ending Violence in Teen Dating Relationships: A Guide for Parents and Pastors.* Minneapolis: Fortress, 2005.

LGBT Issues (for parents and teens)

COLAGE—People with a Lesbian, Gay, Bisexual, Transgender, or Queer Parent. http://www.colage.org.

Huegel, Kelly. *GLBTQ: The Survival Guide for Gay, Lesbian, Bisexual, Transgender, and Questioning Teens.* Minneapolis: Free Spirit, 2012.

PFLAG—Parents, Families, and Friends of Lesbians and Gays. http://www.pflag.org.

Savage, Dan, and Terry Miller, eds. *It Gets Better: Coming Out, Overcoming Bullying, and Creating a Life Worth Living.* New York: Penguin, 2012.

TransFaith. http://www.transfaithonline.org. This is a national, nonprofit organization that is led by transgendered people and is focused on issues of faith and spirituality.

Teen Pregnancy

The National Campaign to Prevent Teen Pregnancy. http://www.thenationalcampaign.org.

U.S. Centers for Disease Control and Prevention. Teen Pregnancy Parent Resources. http://www.cdc.gov/TeenPregnancy/Parents.htm.

Disability

National Dissemination Center for Students with Disabilities. Sex Education for Students with Disabilities. http://nichcy.org/schools-administrators/sexed.

Schwier, Karin Melberg, and Dave Hingsburger. *Sexuality: Your Sons and Daughters with Intellectual Disabilities*. Baltimore: Paul H. Brookes Co., 2000.

Technology

Common Sense Media. http://www.commonsensemedia.org/.

Connect Safely. http://www.connectsafely.org/.

Boyd, Dana. Apophenia. http://www.zephoria.org/thoughts/. This is a technology-use blog featuring up-to-date studies and information on children, teen, and adult use of technology.

Resources for Children and Youth

Birth to Kindergarten

Harris, Robbie H., and Michael Emberley. *It's NOT the Stork! A Book about Girls, Boys, Babies, Bodies, Families, and Friends*. Somerville, MA: Candlewick, 2008.

King, Kimberly, and Sue Rama. *I Said No! A Kid-to-Kid Guide to Keeping Your Private Parts Private*. Weaverville, CA: Boulden, 2008.

Saltz, Gail. *Amazing You! Getting Smart about Your Private Parts*. New York: Puffin, 2008.

Elementary Years

Cole, Joanna. *Asking about Sex and Growing Up: A Question-and-Answer Book for Kids*. Rev. ed. New York: Harper Collins, 2009.

Harris, Robbie H., and Michael Emberley. *It's So Amazing! A Book about Eggs, Sperm, Birth, Babies, and Families*. Somerville, MA: Candlewick, 2004.

Madaras, Lynda, and Area Madaras. *My Body, My Self for Boys.* What's Happening to My Body? Rev. ed. New York: New Market, 2007.

Madaras, Lynda. *My Body, My Self for Girls.* A What's Happening to My Body? New York: New Market, 2007.

Tween Years

Harris, Robbie H., and Michael Emberley. *It's Perfectly Normal: Changing Bodies, Growing Up, Sex, and Sexual Health.* Somerville, MA: Candlewick, 2009.

Gravelle, Karen, with Nick and Chava Castro. *What's Going on Down There? Answers to Questions Boys Find Hard to Ask.* New York: Walker and Company, 1998.

Madaras, Lynda, and Area Madaras. *The What's Happening to My Body? Book for Boys.* 3rd ed. New York: New Market, 2000.

Madaras, Lynda, and Area Madaras. *The What's Happening to My Body? Book for Girls.* 3rd ed. New York: New Market, 2007.

Teen Years

Advocates for Youth. http://www.advocatesforyouth.org.

Corinna, Heather. *S.E.X.: The All-You-Need-to-Know Progressive Sexuality Guide to Get You through High School and College.* New York: Marlowe and Company, 2007.

Duffy, Michael F. *Making Sense of Sex: Responsible Decision Making for Young Singles.* Louisville, KY: Westminster John Knox, 2011.

Love Is Respect.org. http://www.loveisrespect.org/. This site also includes a dating abuse hotline.

Mark D. Regnerus, *Forbidden Fruit: Sex and Religion in the Lives of American Teenagers.* New York: Oxford University Press, 2007.

Sex, Etc. http://www.sexetc.org/. This is a sexuality education site by teens, for teens.

List of Question Boxes

Questions and Statements from Children

About the Body

About Sexual Intercourse

About Faith

About Family and Relationships

About Gender Identity and Sexual Orientation

Index

sexual orientation, 22–23, 78, 130–32. *See also* homosexuality; sexual identity

sexuality
categories of, 19–20
faith and, ix, xi
informing about, 4–5, 9, 20–22

sexuality education
answering kids' questions for, 31–33 (*See also List of Question Boxes, pp. 157-59*)
meaning of, 18
parents' role in, 4–7

sexualization, 19–20. *See also* bullying; media literacy

sexually transmited infections (STIs), 4, 15, 19, 120–22, 124, 128, 136

sperm production, 94. *See also* semenarche; spermarche

spermarche, 26, 70, 91, 93, 119. *See also* puberty

stewardship, 9–11

Sunday school, 53–34, 56, 134

"talk, the," 6

technology, 106–7, 122. *See also* Facebook; media literacy

toddlers, 41–42

touch, 39–44, 110–11

transgender, 23

transitional objects, 53

trust, developing, 47–48

TV shows. *See* media literacy

values
learning, 56, 108–9
ownership of, 140
shared, 77
stories as examples of, 57
See also beliefs; faith

virginity pledges, 128. *See also* abstinence-only-until-marriage

worship attendance, 55, 80. *See also* membership, church

CPSIA information can be obtained at www.ICGtesting.com
Printed in the USA
BVOW01s0016300913

332323BV00006B/15/P

9 780664 237998